Over, Under, Around, and Through

How Hall of Famers Surmount Obstacles

Jill S. Tietjen, PE *&*
Elinor Miller Greenberg, EdD

FULCRUM
Wheat Ridge, Colorado

Library of Congress Cataloging-in-Publication Data

Names: Tietjen, Jill S., author. | Greenberg, Elinor, author.
Title: Over, under, around, and through : how hall of famers surmount obstacles / Jill S. Tietjen, PE, Elinor Miller Greenberg, EdD.
Description: Wheat Ridge, Colorado : Fulcrum Publishing, [2022] | Includes bibliographical references.
Identifiers: LCCN 2021035806 | ISBN 9781682753354 (paperback)
Subjects: LCSH: Success--Psychological aspects. | Goal (Psychology) | Successful people--Anecdotes. | Women--Anecdotes. | Colorado Women's Hall of Fame.
Classification: LCC BF637.S8 T37 2022 | DDC 158.1082--dc23
LC record available at https://lccn.loc.gov/2021035806

Printed in the United States
0 9 8 7 6 5 4 3 2 1

Fulcrum Publishing
3970 Youngfield Street
Wheat Ridge, Colorado 80033
(800) 992-2908 • (303) 277-1623
www.fulcrumbooks.com

*In Memory
of Elinor Miller Greenberg
1932–2021*

Contents

Foreword

by Marilyn Van Derbur Atler

When I was a nineteen-year-old sophomore at the University of Colorado, my life took a life-altering turn. In April, I was chosen Miss University of Colorado. In September, I was Miss America. One of Miss America's jobs was to go to different cities to help celebrate their most important days or events. Every day, I would meet the most outstanding people of the community, and

Marilyn Van Derbur Atler

I was asked multiple times each day to "speak a few words." At first I had no idea what I was going to say, but after a few appearances, my passion was ignited. I knew I was going to be a motivational speaker.

It became my passion to learn about success, goals, natural ability, and persistence.

Jill and Ellie share my passion and have written an amazing book about successful women. I couldn't put the book down. I hope as you are reading, you will think about yourself. Your successes and failures. Your hopes and dreams.

Let me give you some information and see how you would "judge" these people – as successes or as failures.

He ran for political office seven times and was defeated each time.

He wanted to publish a children's book. It was rejected by publishers fifty-four times.

In trying to solve a problem, she tried 487 different experiments, all of which failed.

He wanted to sketch and cartoon. He applied for a job with a Kansas City newspaper. After looking at his work, the editor said, "To be frank with you, it's easy to see from these sketches that you have no talent."

She wanted to be Miss America. She entered the pageant three times and lost.

🏵 🏵 🏵

Abraham Lincoln was defeated for legislature, defeated for speaker, defeated for nomination to Congress, defeated for reelection to Congress, rejected for land officer, defeated again for Senate, defeated for nomination as vice president, and again defeated for Senate. In 1860, he was elected president of the United States. Was Abraham Lincoln a success or a failure? He was both.

After he was turned down by fifty-four publishers, a friend of his at Vanguard Press decided to take a chance on him, and at age thirty-three, Ted Geisel (Dr. Seuss) had his first book, *And to Think That I Saw It on Mulberry Street*, published. Although his books were never very thick, it took him an average of a year to write one, and he estimated that he wrote and drew more than one thousand pages for every sixty-four pages that were finally used in each book.

After trying an experiment 487 times to try to isolate radium, Madame Curie's husband threw up his hands and said, "It will never be done. Maybe in one hundred years but never in our day."

She replied, "If it takes one hundred years, it will be a pity but I will not cease working for it as long as I live." She was successful, and she was the first woman to win a Nobel Prize, and the only woman to win two.

His dream was to sketch and cartoon. He went from studio to studio, always being turned down. Finally, he got a job drawing publicity material for a church. He couldn't afford an office so he rented an old dilapidated garage that was infested with mice. As he would sketch, the mice would run back and forth as he tried to concentrate. Thirty years later, Walt Disney was world famous, and so was one of the mice!

Laurie Schaefer wanted to be Miss America. The first time she competed, she didn't even place in the final ten. Her sophomore year of college, she entered again. She placed in the final ten, but not in the final five. The next year she was the second runner-up. In front of her family and friends, she had lost again. Two days after the pageant, a state official called her and said, "The judges didn't understand the balloting. We've recounted the ballots and you won . . . but . . . it's already been publicly announced. There's nothing we can do about it." What did she do? Run to the newspapers and say, "I really won"? The state official said, "Would you try one more time?" Laurie said to me, "I'll never forget how hesitant I was to reenter a pageant I had won, but once I set my mind to something I keep trying over and over until that goal is fulfilled." So, she entered the Miss Ohio Pageant for the fourth time, and she then went on to become Miss America.

Former Miss Americas Donna Axum and Heather French both entered the pageant four years in a row before winning.

Joe Biden ran for president three times. President Ronald Reagan ran for president in 1968 and 1976 before winning in 1980.

President Franklin Roosevelt failed the bar exam on the first try, as did John F. Kennedy, Jr., Michelle Obama, Secretary of State Hillary Clinton, Governor Jerry Brown, Mayors Ed Koch and Richard Daley, and countless others.

During an NFL Draft, Tom Brady was the 199th pick.

Does the best man win? Is it the brightest student who gets the best job? Is it the prettiest girl who wins the contest? I wasn't even the prettiest girl *in my family*!

As I studied successful men's and women's lives, I found that failure never stopped one of them. Another theme I kept finding is how disciplined successful people are.

When I was producing a motivational video, I wanted to talk about Ayn Rand. I wrote to her, requesting a picture. Her personal response is a treasured letter.

She is one of America's best-known authors. When she wrote *The Fountainhead*, she wanted to probe the importance of the individual. She decided the best way she could develop this theme was through a man she would call Howard Roark, who stood by his personal ideals at all costs. She chose architecture as his profession. *For two years, before she had written one word*, Ayn plunged into the history of architecture, the aesthetics, and architectural engineering. She read professional journals and biographies of architects. Finally, she felt she was ready for practical experience, so she went to work in an architect's office. Only the man who hired her knew that her real purpose in working there was research for a novel. It took her seven years to write *The Fountainhead*. Some years later, Ayn met Frank Lloyd Wright – the most famous architect in America. He said, "I've read every word of your book. Your grasp of architecture astonishes me."

It took Ayn thirteen years to write *Atlas Shrugged*. Does that mean she would write for a few hours a day, a couple of days a week? No. She drove herself at a ruthless pace. She worked seven days a week. It was not unusual for her to eat dinner at midnight. There was one period of intense work when she did not step out of her apartment for thirty-three days.

Ernest Hemingway rewrote the last chapter to *A Farewell to Arms* thirty-nine times. Sometimes he would spend an entire morning on one paragraph.

John Steinbeck (winner of the Nobel Prize in Literature) wrote to a friend, "I finished my novel and let it stand for a while, then read it over. It is no good. Even to the last page, I thought it was going to be good and it is not." Several years later he wrote, "I do not write easily. Three hours of writing requires twenty hours of preparation. Rejection follows rejection. There have been no encouraging letters."

Discipline. Persistence.

As a competitive swimmer myself, I have always followed Olympic swimmers with great interest. Shane Gould wanted to be an Olympic champion; she has been called the greatest swimmer Australia has ever produced. By age fifteen, she had set every world's freestyle swimming record for women. She got up at 4:15 every morning – not just the mornings she felt like it. When she hit the water at 5:15, she could tell you exactly how many laps she was going to swim. Freestyle, backstroke, breaststroke. For example: Shane would swim 800 meters freestyle for a warm-up – that would be approximately the same as swimming the length of eight football fields without stopping. She swam 352 laps. She would be back in the pool after school at four and swim until six with an even more strenuous workout. She could tell you when she was going to study. Fifteen minutes here – ten minutes there. Every minute was accounted for. It was an extreme plan, but she had an extreme goal. Shane wanted to be the best in the world. And she was.

Discipline. Persistence.

I know about discipline and persistence. When I was thirty-eight, I was named the Outstanding Woman Speaker in America. A rabbit could have won that award if she had worked as hard as I did. I spent hundreds of hours on one speech. Every word had to be perfect. Every single example had to convey a message to the audience. I have given literally thousands of speeches. One year, before my daughter was born, I was addressing three high school assemblies during the day and a banquet at night. Speaking in two different cities in one day was common.

I was driven. I was driven to be perfect. Because beneath the Miss America facade, beneath the outstanding speaker, lurked pain beyond description. Beyond description.

Another theme I saw when researching successful people was that many came from very challenging backgrounds, but they didn't let that stop them.

It isn't what happens to us that determines our lives, it's how we respond to what happens.

My father started coming into my bedroom when I was five. He didn't stop until I left for college at eighteen. I would pull myself into the tightest fetal position my body could tighten into and stay as quiet as I could. He would always come home around nine. My room was above the garage door. I would wait and wait and wait. My body seemed to be all ears. Listening, listening for the doorknob to turn. Sometime the nights he didn't come were as difficult as the nights he did come. I buried DEEPLY all of the feelings I was not allowed to express. Humiliation. Anger. Helplessness. Hopelessness. The problem is – when you bury feelings alive, they just sit there until something triggers them. The feelings come up as if they are happening in real time. As the feelings began pushing up from my subconscious, my conscious mind fought with every ounce of energy to keep the feelings down.

When my daughter turned five, my horrifically conflicted body went into physical paralysis. I was hospitalized for the better part of three months. Doctors in Denver could find no cause. The Mayo Clinic could find no cause. One day it flashed into my mind. Jennifer's *age* is triggering this. When she was turning thirteen, I had a complete, total breakdown. It's called "recovery." Deep, deep, endless sobbing, body tightness like piano wire, overwhelming shame. The only way to stop the craziness of my mind and body was to no longer stuff the feelings – to bring them up and feel them as if it were happening to me in real time. I was in intense therapy for six years, until Jennifer turned eighteen.

One day a therapist said to me, "You must stop closing and locking your bedroom door. You are just repatterning the nights. *Leave your door open.*" I could not believe what she was asking. I *had to lock my bedroom door.* I couldn't even imagine trying to sleep with my door open. He would come in the night. He always came in the night. The first night I left the door open and I jumped into bed – for about one minute. I closed and locked the door. The second night the same thing. I so wanted to be "well." I so wanted to get the memories and the feelings up and out and return to my life. But if I left my door open, I would die. I don't ask you – the reader – to understand that feeling, I only ask that you honor the fact that

that was my belief. The third night, I left the door open. I turned on my side with my face away from the door. I curled up into the tightest fetal position possible, and then I said to myself, "If I die, I die, but I don't want to live this way anymore."

Sometimes we have to walk right into the terror. *Sometimes we have to do the thing we fear the most in order to succeed.*

Having "my story" on the cover of *People* magazine was *my worst nightmare – I thought.* Actually, it became one of my greatest blessings. I have spoken in more than five hundred cities. I have been in touch with more adult survivors of rape/sexual assault than anyone in America. What a privilege it has been to help men and women face their traumas, release their shame, and begin living authentic lives.

If you've ever thought about yourself as a failure, remember you're not alone – failure and rejection are a part of everyone's life.

After hearing me speak, a young girl wrote to me, "It takes guts to stay involved in life – to find your way – to find where you fit in this world."

As you read about these amazing women Jill and Ellie have written about, think of your own life. What are *your* goals? If you don't succeed on your first try, will you try again? What physical, emotional, intellectual challenges are you willing to take on to make *your* dreams come true?

– Marilyn Van Derbur Atler
Former Miss America
www.MissAmericaByDay.com
Colorado Authors' Hall of Fame
Colorado Women's Hall of Fame

Preface

We, Jill and Ellie, had talked about doing a book together for many years. It took the 2020 COVID-19 pandemic and an International Women's Forum – Colorado Wine-Around (a virtual happy hour) to give us the spark of an idea.

All humans face obstacles (which we originally referred to as "puddles" as we thought about the book title and approach) in their lives. The inductees into the Colorado Women's Hall of Fame, including the two of us, are no exception. We have come to believe that each inductee, as accomplished as she might be, has had to overcome multiple obstacles on her life's journey. Each has had to learn behaviors and attitudes along the way that helped her become successful.

Ellie demonstrated one of her attitudes during our initial discussion on her back patio when Jill asked Ellie what she had done when she confronted an obstacle. Ellie used a little hand motion showing that she had gone around the obstacle, around the "puddle." To Jill, that said it all: the inductees didn't see obstacles as immovable, impossible barriers – there were ways around, over, under, or sometimes even through the puddles.

We also have come to believe that many people around the world might be able to benefit from hearing these women's stories and might garner inspiration from other women in order to deal with the obstacles in their own lives. And thus our work together began on this book project – over a stay-at-home summer lunch on Ellie's back patio, as we sought to keep some semblance of social distancing from each other as required by the pandemic.

The next step was to schedule interviews with the Colorado Women's Hall of Fame inductees in order to gather the material for our book. Sister Lydia Peña, one of our interviewees, added words of encouragement for our project: "All the best with this special project that will, no doubt, benefit many. The young ones who think that successful people never meet up with 'puddles,' and older women who understand that if there are no 'puddles,' there is not life." Thank you, Sister Lydia.

The inductees related stories of professional and personal obstacles they had encountered. Some were heartrending. All were life determining. We thank them from the bottom of our hearts for their honesty and their intimacy in sharing those stories.

We also researched historical inductees, the obstacles they had faced, and the skills they used to surmount those obstacles. We interlaced their stories with those of the contemporary inductees.

We believe that the reader will come to understand that all of us face obstacles – the key is how we react to them and what we learn in confronting and overcoming. Over and over again, these women faced down obstacles, puddles, determined that they would overcome them, as they persisted in moving forward. They didn't always keep their feet dry, but they tried.

Acknowledgments

No one writes a book alone. Many, many people provide support, guidance, direction, and input. We apologize in advance for any omissions in this list, however unintended.

To Jill Wright whose comment at the Virtual Wine Around sparked the idea for the book topic.

To the board of the Colorado Women's Hall of Fame and former board chairs Beth Barela and Betty Heid. Thank you.

We were fortunate to have the opportunity to interview so many inductees into the Colorado Women's Hall of Fame. We thank them for their time, candor, and sharing. Christine Arguello, Marilyn Van Derbur Atler, Polly Baca, Merle Chambers, Sister Alicia Cuarón, Terri Finkel, Patricia Gabow, Temple Grandin, Maria Guajardo, Penny Hamilton, Bee Harris, Josie Heath, Susan Helms, Arlene Hirschfeld, Dorothy Horrell, Ding-Wen Hsu, Jo Ann Joselyn, Dottie Lamm, Carlotta Walls LaNier, Mary Lou Makepeace, Mary Mullarkey, Carol Mutter, LaRae Orullian, Sister Lydia Peña, Cleo Parker Robinson, Pat Schroeder, Shari Shink, Martha Urioste, and Diana Wall.

To Enid Ablowitz and Ann Kellan who provided guidance on the book title as well as support and encouragement.

To Alison Auch and Sam Scinta and the rest of the staff at Fulcrum Publishing who understood the book concept and helped make the book better.

To Jill's husband, David Tietjen, who always supports my many endeavors.

And, to Ellie's children, Michael, Andrea, and Julie, who helped get the book across the finish line.

Introduction

I have learned that success is to be measured
not so much by the position that one has achieved in life
as by the obstacles which he has overcome
while trying to succeed.
– Booker T. Washington

All of us face obstacles in our lives. Some of those obstacles are readily overcome, but others take years to conquer and recover from. For many people, the obstacles themselves, and the manner in which they may overcome those obstacles – over, under, around, or through – become life defining.

We may think that successful people don't face obstacles in their lives. The opposite is true. Successful people usually have faced and overcome many obstacles, and they do it with a variety of strategies, often unthinkingly, but sometimes extremely deliberately and consciously.

For more than fifty years now, we have had the opportunity to read hundreds, perhaps thousands, of books and articles about "how women succeed," "how women should dress for success," "how women can have successful careers and marriages too," and other topics focusing on "successful" women. These books and articles have been timely and very helpful. They have often guided women in their development and their searches for models of contemporary life, especially those models that show how women can combine their careers with successful and healthy family lives. In some cases, these writings have actually saved marriages. In others, careers have been enhanced by various tips and suggestions from others.

Now that we have had at least one generation of experience with millions of contemporary women who have successfully combined their working lives with their family lives, it is time to more fully explore the *challenges* and the *obstacles* that so-called successful women have faced and overcome, as they have pioneered these new, contemporary models of living.

One would expect that if someone had been inducted into the Colorado (or any state's) Women's Hall of Fame, they would have achieved something quite special. And, they would likely be considered successful and might also be prominent and well-known. Their life stories might be included in a *Who's Who* publication, or they might have been the subject of a film. They might be popular speakers at various local and perhaps national or even international events. Perhaps, they themselves have written an autobiographical book or have had the opportunity to make a film or TV program about their own lives.

So it was with the many exceptional women who have been inducted into the Colorado Women's Hall of Fame and who we interviewed for this book. These prominent women have often been held up as role models for others. They are accustomed to being portrayed as successful, as having it all, and as being thought of as worthy of being emulated by others. We interlace the stories from the current inductees into the hall with stories from those who are no longer with us.

But, the truth is that the sailing has not always been smooth for these women – contemporary or historical. In conceiving this book, we believed that if we dug deeply into these women's life stories, we would find serious obstacles, or "puddles," that they had confronted and had to overcome.

We also believed that these puddles were not publicly known, were often hidden from view, and were rarely publicly discussed. They were not usually the subjects of written reports, speeches, or other narratives. In addition, we thought that these very puddles might have been the actual challenges that spurred these women on toward their successes. Maybe it was the challenges, the actual difficulties, that became the catalysts for constructive and creative action!

It therefore became intriguing to find out if we could identify the challenges these successful women faced; and then, we thought, we might be able to discover how they met and surmounted them. In doing so, we thought we might be able to provide other women and girls – and men and boys – with various lessons learned and rules of the road, as they, too, met the inevitable challenges in their own unfolding lives.

Based on our interviews, coupled with our review of the relevant literature, we have identified ten key characteristics that are usually exhibited by so-called successful people. Those ten key characteristics are:

1. Mental Intelligence
2. Emotional Intelligence
3. Social Support
4. Moral Compass – Spirituality
5. Determination – Perseverance – Persistence
6. Optimism

7. Creativity

8. Resilience

9. Action-Orientation

10. Passion

In the following chapters, we define each of these ten key characteristics and tell the stories that demonstrate and exemplify how these successful women overcame obstacles and went on to lead remarkable lives. Although each woman's story appears in one chapter and is associated with one of these ten characteristics, often more than one characteristic was called upon in order to surmount an obstacle.

These successful women all experienced significant challenges along the way. It was often overcoming those challenges and learning the lessons those challenges presented that paved the way for the success each woman experienced. We hope that as you read this book and the stories contained herein, you will be inspired and motivated to face the obstacles in your life and reach for the stars.

CHAPTER 1

Mental Intelligence

Mental intelligence involves acquiring and applying one's knowledge and skills to solve problems, address new and difficult situations, perform reasoning activities, and conduct critical thinking. Tests have been developed to measure mental intelligence – these tests measure IQ, the intelligence quotient, relating to intellectual functioning.

People who score well on intelligence tests are often referred to in our culture as "smart" and generally learn from their experiences, are able to adapt to new circumstances, can handle abstract concepts, and are able to manipulate their environment. They are usually curious and are able to put ideas together to solve problems.

The women in this chapter used their mental intelligence to demonstrate their capabilities, solve problems, and directly address the obstacles that arose in their lives.

Health to Match Our Mountains –
Dr. Florence Sabin

At the age of seventy-three, when "the nice, retired lady doctor," Dr. Florence Sabin, was asked to head the Colorado State Health Committee, she was the nation's foremost woman scientist with a long list of firsts. She spearheaded the revision of Colorado's health statutes for the first time in seventy-one years, completely shook up the state's Health Department, and led the way to Coloradans having levels of "Health to Match Our Mountains."

Descended from a line of male doctors, Florence's mental intelligence was obvious from a young age. After her mother died when she was just seven, she and her sister, Mary, first went to a private boarding school in Denver, then one in Chicago, and then another in Vermont. At Smith College, Florence was encouraged to study medicine by her mentor and counselor, despite the fact that American medical schools were not accepting women, and the silver panic of 1893 meant her father couldn't pay for medical school.

Florence was not deterred! She worked as a teacher to earn the money for medical school and became one of the first woman students at Johns Hopkins University Medical School – whose benefactors had demanded that women be accepted. Her model of a newborn baby's brain was used by generations of neurology students. Her 1901 *Atlas of the Midbrain and Medulla* became a widely used and valued medical text. She became a full professor – the first woman professor at the medical school. Florence's many other firsts include the first woman member of the National Academy of Sciences.

The "leading woman scientist in the world" retired to Denver in 1938. But in 1946, at age seventy-three, she agreed to head the State Health Committee to revise Colorado's health laws, which were still the same as they had been at the time of statehood, in 1876. Her eight Sabin health bills didn't pass the legislature under the governor that appointed her, but the next governor supported them, and she became the director of the new State Board of Health.

Dr. Florence Sabin

But Florence wasn't done. As manager of the Denver Department of Health and Charities, she helped establish a city-wide program to diagnose tuberculosis. She spearheaded efforts to remove rats from the city's alleys and dump. She finally retired permanently when she was eighty years old.

Each state is allotted two statues in Statuary Hall in the US Capitol. Dr. Florence Sabin, whose legacy, "Health to Match Our Mountains," improved the health of all the people of Colorado, is enshrined there.

Work Harder, Work Smarter –
Temple Grandin

As an unconventional woman and a pioneer in a male-dominated business and role, animal scientist Temple Grandin had to work twice as hard and be twice as smart as the men in her field in order to be credible.

In the 1970s, when she started in the animal science industry, she says that being a woman was a much bigger obstacle than her autism had ever been. Before she had established herself as an expert on cattle behavior and handling, and before her chutes and other designs were commonplace at feed lots, bull testicles were put on her vehicle at a cattle handling facility. At that point, she decided she had to make herself credible. So she went to the editor of the *Arizona Farmer Ranchman* magazine and began to write articles. Once her expertise was established publicly, she knew she would have to be admitted to the feed lots.

Temple developed the reputation of being a good reporter. At her first cattle feeders meeting in Arizona, she wasn't going to be admitted because she was a woman. But she cajoled the guard until he let her in. Then she wrote an excellent article summarizing the various speakers. That's the way she built a reputation for writing well and for being accurate in her coverage of meetings.

When Temple was given a project to put in a dip vat (used to remove external parasites from cattle) for one of her clients, she estimates that her knowledge of the project was about 60 percent. She didn't know how to do the concrete work. Her solution was to use her mental intelligence to acquire the knowledge she needed, after which she was able to complete the project satisfactorily.

Temple Grandin.
Photo by Rosalie Winard.

Temple believes that her autism drove her to prove that she "wasn't stupid" and that she could do good work. When she was told that she couldn't do something, she felt incredibly motivated to prove that the speaker was wrong and that she could do the task. She was also always motivated to do her "very, very best." Whenever there was another hurdle for her to conquer, Temple conquered it by working harder and working smarter.

Ladies Day at Harvard Law School –
Mary Mullarkey

The first woman chief justice of the Colorado Supreme Court, Mary Mullarkey, wasn't always welcomed or valued in the legal profession. But having only brothers and a mother who had aspired to be a lawyer – although she herself was precluded from doing so – Mary was able to shine throughout her career.

Entering Harvard Law School in 1965, Mary was told by male classmates that she was "taking the place of a male student who had been killed in Vietnam." Male professors had still not adjusted to the idea of having women in law school, although at the time, about 5 percent of the students in Mary's class were women. The property law class professor was particularly unwelcoming, allowing women students the opportunity to participate in class only one day during the entire year of the class – the so-called Ladies Day – even though the students' responses to questions were an important part of their legal education and their grades.

Growing up with four brothers absolutely influenced Mary's self-esteem. She was used to being in the minority and being teased. In addition, although neither of her parents had gone to college, they always spoke to their children of "*when* you go to college," not "*if* you go to college." Her mother had wanted to go to law school. She had actually applied and been accepted in the days before a college education was a requirement for admission. However, Mary's maternal grandmother refused to allow such a thing! But Mary's mother had a good legal mind, and Mary grew up hearing about her mother's work for a district attorney. Mary demonstrated her mental intelligence when she took the LSAT, the exam required for admission to law schools in the United States. Her scores were excellent, and when she applied to Harvard Law School, she was

Mary Mullarkey

accepted. When she wrote to tell Harvard that she could not afford to attend, Harvard responded with an offer of financial aid that included scholarships and work-study programs.

Although Harvard Law School was welcoming from an administrative standpoint, the professors and her classmates were not consistently friendly. Mary said that she would have learned a lot more if she had been treated better in law school. Former chief justice Mary Mullarkey concluded that "a 'Ladies Day' alone does not a welcoming environment provide!"

CHAPTER 2

Emotional Intelligence

Emotional intelligence is deemed to be critical to having personal and professional success. It is the ability to handle one's own emotions and to relate appropriately and empathetically with others. The four categories of emotional intelligence are self-awareness, self-management, social awareness, and relationship management.

Someone who is self-aware understands her own emotions and her reactions to situations. She also is aware of how her behavior drives the behaviors of others. Self-management refers to the ability to control and adapt one's emotions and behaviors to situations and as situations evolve. Social awareness means that people understand how situations affect the people around them. These people look for cues, including language and nonverbal behavior, to assess circumstances in which they find themselves. Relationship management means that an individual understands her own emotions and behaviors as well as the emotions and behaviors of others and uses that information to have good relationships with other people.

People with high emotional intelligence know how they feel and how others feel and are thus able to adjust their behavior to a particular situation.

The women featured in this chapter used their understanding of people to succeed and surmount their challenges.

Everybody Welcome –
Fannie Mae Duncan

Fannie Mae Duncan learned while working at her family's fruit stand in Oklahoma that you always treated paying customers with respect. She applied her emotional intelligence when she ran the Cotton Club, in Colorado Springs, Colorado, during an era of de facto segregation. After she was told by the police chief to admit only African American customers, her non-Black customers rebelled and complained to him. He reversed his stance, and Fannie Mae was able to again put up her sign that said, "Everybody Welcome."

The granddaughter of slaves and the first in her family to graduate from high school, Fannie Mae overcame her father's death when she was young and many years of working at menial jobs to become an entrepreneur in Colorado Springs. Her family moved to Guthrie, Oklahoma, from Alabama before she was born, and her years in Guthrie enabled her to demonstrate her quick mind. Her father let her make change at their fruit stand because of her excellent math skills. After his death, her family moved to Colorado, where opportunities were provided to her by other family members so she could both work and go to school.

When Fannie Mae heard jazz greats in Denver and realized that they would come to Colorado Springs to perform if they were provided with a venue and paying customers, she established the

Cotton Club. It became very popular. It was also an integrated establishment – the first in Colorado Springs. When the police chief requested that she not run an integrated operation, she said, "You didn't tell me to check for color." Because she offered a club that was easy to find, had good food, provided outstanding entertainment, and was "hard to leave," her many customers of all races and ethnicities rallied to

Fannie Mae Duncan

her cause. She welcomed everybody, and the police chief eventually became one of her biggest supporters.

Fannie Mae opened new doors for society and for women. Her sign, "Everybody Welcome," left a legacy for how people from different walks of life can come together.

There's No Challenge Too Great –
Gudy Gaskill

The Colorado Trail, more than 550 miles from Denver to Durango, Colorado, would not have happened without Gudy Gaskill. Its completion reflected her philosophy: "There's no challenge too great that you can't overcome, if you really become bold and do not believe the answer no."

Gudy overcame the male-dominated US Forest Service, the male-dominated mountaineering clubs in Colorado, and nature itself to organize the volunteers who made the Colorado Trail a reality. It was said of her that she led with determination, with vision, with creativity, and from her heart. And based on her emotional intelligence, people wanted to work with her because she made it clear to them what benefits they would derive from the effort.

Her backbone, and also her capacity for positivity and finding the best in people, emerged from a very difficult childhood. Her father was very controlling, and her mother was very submissive. When Gudy encouraged her mother to be more aggressive in dealing with her father, Gudy was punished. She decided, however, to emerge positively from that experience. As a result, she has been described as "attracting people like honey attracts bees."

A woman with almost endless energy, Gudy painted watercolors of nature's beauty. She taught herself pottery. She believed she could set her mind to do something, and then she could learn how to do it.

Gudy Gaskill

When she set her mind on building the Colorado Trail, it got done. She found and organized the volunteers. She wrote grant proposals to acquire the funding for the materials and to feed the volunteers. She welcomed the volunteer groups when they arrived to work for the weekend. She cooked for them, she cleaned up, and she thanked them – she gave them watercolors she had painted, poems she had written, and pottery she had crafted.

Gudy didn't know that the Colorado Trail would become a model for other projects around the world, as well as an attraction for tourists from outside of Colorado. She just knew she wanted to share her love of nature and the beauty of the state. And, she found there was "no challenge too great that you can't overcome."

Going Out on a Limb –
Ding-Wen Hsu

Ding-Wen Hsu didn't even think about the risks when she decided to plan Denver's Dragon Boat Festival. Her goal was to pull together the pan-Asian community in Colorado, so she put together a team and a project plan, and "off they went." Only on the morning of the inaugural event did it occur to her that people might not show up. But, instead of the three thousand people they had promised the vendors, fifteen thousand people showed up! "Going out on a limb" paid off for her because she had assembled just the right team.

Ding had originally thought the Dragon Boat Festival would be mainly for the Chinese community in Colorado. An examination of the limited resources in the Chinese community, however, showed that it needed to be a pan-Asian event. The idea of an event for the pan-Asian community was so exciting to Ding that she went out and started talking to a variety of people to help her plan it. Her enthusiasm was contagious, and she was able to assemble a great diverse team that supported her vision.

Ding not only put the program plan together, but while staying in charge, she demonstrated her emotional intelligence and gave the volunteers working on the project their very own part of it. Each volunteer was allowed to select an area that interested them, and then they were allowed to conduct their work reasonably autonomously.

The Dragon Boat Festival also taught Ding that she had leadership skills and that she should not be shy about using them. In addition, the project identified a great deal of talent in the Asian community. As a result, a Young Leaders Program was established to train the next generation of leaders.

Ding-Wen Hsu

Ding said that the Dragon Boat Festival experience taught her to trust people. The team she had – that she had basically selected – delivered on what they promised to do. It also taught her to take risks – to "go out on that limb" – and to not be afraid.

I've Got a PhD in White People –
Carlotta Walls LaNier

The youngest of the Little Rock Nine, Carlotta Walls LaNier was fourteen years old when she became one of the nine Black students who in 1957 integrated Central High School in Little Rock, Arkansas. Building on the strong foundation she received from her extended family and her emotional intelligence, she survived that incredibly difficult experience, which played out on national television. As a result, Carlotta says that she developed trust in herself, as well the ability to read other people and their motivations, particularly white people. She says that she "has her PhD in white people."

Carlotta believes that she sat at the foot of the greats growing up – her great-aunts and -uncles and grandparents. Raised in an era where children could be seen but not heard, she listened intently to what was being said, and she learned. She was told that "she was just as good as the next person." She was taught that there were a lot of things that are not fair or are not right in life and that those things were being challenged and changed. She learned how to address people and how to get others to hear what she was saying. And she learned to help others in her church and in her community.

Carlotta says she didn't want to have anyone hurt because of her decision to seek a good education at the previously all-white Central High School in Little Rock. She kept a lot of things to herself so her family wouldn't know about all the kinds of trauma she was experiencing. She was taunted daily. There was no one with whom to do homework. She had no friends at the school. Yet she learned to trust herself, and she knew that she could always rely on herself. Other people didn't have to like her, but she did want them to respect her.

Carlotta Walls LaNier

Carlotta believes that white people have ungrounded fears about people of color, and about Black people in particular. Carlotta is certain that once white people get to know someone who doesn't look like them, they begin to relax and lose their fear of knowing other people and other cultures. She would like white people to at least "get a GED in Black people," and to simply be humane in their responses toward the next person. And, she really believes that, over the course of her lifetime, she has "gotten a PhD in white people."

If You Have a Gift and Don't Use It, No Confessor on Earth Can Absolve You – *Dr. Patty Gabow*

The long-standing CEO of Denver Health, Dr. Patty Gabow, was a medical pioneer throughout her career. She describes herself as "a fearless person" who received significant life lessons from her step-father and her grandfather. Those life lessons and her emotional intelligence combined to make her a beloved and effective leader at Denver Health (Denver's public health and hospital system) for twenty years.

Patty's father was killed in World War II when she was only one year old, and a significant number of her formative years were spent living in her maternal grandparents' home. Her grandfather believed strongly that if you have a gift and don't use it, no confessor on Earth can absolve you. This very strong language, instilled in her Catholic upbringing, led Patty to ensure she was always maximizing the use of her talents. That language, combined with her stepfather's directives when she was a student in his high school history class – "Sit in the front row, do your homework, and always raise your hand" – helped to inform her life choices.

Patty raised her hand often, and always used her talents. When she arrived at what was then Denver General Hospital, she was the only woman in the Department of Medicine and the only woman in her department at the University of Colorado School of Medicine. She rose to become chief medical officer under a management team that did not align with her values. But, because she loved the people at the hospital and its mission, she thought long and hard about her alternatives and decided to stay.

Dr. Patty Gabow

When she became CEO a few years later, Patty was able to re-build trust based on a foundation of integrity. During her term as CEO, the hospital was taken out of city government and formed into an independent authority. None of these steps would have been possible without her leadership and ability to build a culture where every employee was valued and acknowledged. She says today that she loved her job and loved the people with whom she worked – all amazing, wonderful, and inspiring people.

Surely, Patty doesn't have to go to confession – she used so well the gifts that she was given.

CHAPTER 3

Social Support

If we did not know it before, we certainly learned during the COVID-19 pandemic that humans are social animals. We need contact with other people, and we need people who care about us – our physical and emotional well-being. Certainly we need a network of family, friends, neighbors, and community members available in times of need to give psychological, physical, and/or financial help. We need people who encourage us.

We want people who model the way for us – they are called role models. These are people who demonstrate behaviors we want to emulate and actions we wish to follow. We want advice – that can come from mentors. From mentors we get answers about how to live our lives, pursue our careers, and integrate our work and family. We want people who advocate for us – those people are called sponsors. We also want a group of friends who are there for us through thick and thin – cheering us on when we succeed, picking us up when we fall, and correcting us when we go wrong.

All of these individuals provide us with **social support**. These close relationships provide us with love and support during good times. And, just as importantly, they provide love and support when we especially need them – during the bad times and times of stress or other difficulty.

The women whose stories are told here found community and strength through social support.

❦ ❦ ❦

Cancer Is Not Catching –
Sue Miller

In 1971, model Sue Miller was devastated when she learned that she had breast cancer. No one would hire her as a model, and her friends deserted her. Eventually, Sue carried cards around with her that said, "Cancer is not catching and we're still beautiful."

Several years after her double mastectomy, Sue was asked to model by a store that sold prostheses. She eventually agreed on the condition that all the models would be breast cancer survivors. Thus was born what would become the "Sue Miller Day of Caring," a nonprofit organization that not only provided fashion shows but also supported breast cancer education and awareness for survivors and their families.

At a time when breast cancer was feared and treatment options were not well developed, breast cancer survivors were often shunned. Thus, Sue Miller provided social support and education when it was badly needed. She had already established a "partner service," through which breast cancer survivors counseled other individuals who were undergoing breast cancer treatment.

Sue lobbied the Colorado State Legislature to require organizations that provided health care to also provide mammograms for all women over forty. She lobbied for federal funding for breast cancer research. And she continued to provide fashion shows with breast cancer survivors as models.

Sue Miller

Her autobiography is entitled *I'm Tougher Than I Look.* Sue directly provided social support and encouragement to so many and left a legacy that provides for similar services to be delivered by others. Truly, she proved that "cancer is not catching" and that she – and others – were still quite beautiful.

Nothing'll Stop the US Air Force –
Susan Helms

Being in the first class of women at the United States Air Force Academy was not an experience for which Susan Helms (retired general) was prepared. The oldest of four girls who grew up in Oregon, Susan was the daughter of a career air force officer. Although she did not have an understanding of the extent of bias against women, she was still delighted that Congress had changed the law to allow women to attend the service academies. She was very excited to have been selected for the first class that included women at the Air Force Academy.

Susan arrived at the academy in Colorado Springs, Colorado, in 1976, 1 of 153 women out of a class of about 1,600. However, as she relates, it was really 153 women with a total male student body of 4,347. Most of those male cadets were not pleased to have women at the academy, particularly since they had expected to have an all-male experience for their entire four years, and they had had less than a year to prepare for the surprise arrival of women.

Fortunately for Susan and the other women in her class, the air force took those nine months to determine how it would house, educate, socialize, and indoctrinate the new women cadets. As a result, a separate living area was set up for the 153 freshmen women – not with their squadron, as was the norm, but with the other women who were just beginning their careers at the academy.

Because of this living arrange-
ment, a strong support system formed
among the women. They all knew
each other, and almost everyone bonded. Since they all lived
together, they had freedom to
maneuver among each other's
rooms. When things got tough,
this strong social support structure always provided someone with
whom each of the women could
commiserate. After that first year,
the women lived with their squadrons. Out of the 153 women who
entered the academy in that first class, 97 women graduated.

Susan Helms

Susan, who had a distinguished career in the US Air Force
and as an astronaut, relates a story that demonstrates the strength
of this social support structure. When she went on her first space
flight, she invited every woman in her class to come to Florida to
watch her launch. Although she could not party with them – she
was quarantined for the week before her flight – she says that about
two-thirds of her class were able to accept her invitation and they
had a heck of a party!

You're Not a Failure –
Dottie Lamm

Former First Lady of Colorado (aka Second Banana) Dottie Lamm found herself in what was probably a clinical depression after losing the 1998 election for the US Senate. She thought she was a failure. Dottie said she spent most of the rest of the fall and winter sleeping and skiing. She watched her family and staff recover and move on to other things, but she was stuck. And she felt like she had the plague – no one would talk to her, and when she went to dinner parties, no one wanted her opinion. It was like she wasn't there.

In the spring of 1999, she got a call from a woman who wanted her to do a breakout session at the Women's Success Forum, a conference being held in downtown Denver. Dottie burst into tears and said, "But I'm not a success! Why do you want me?" The woman on the other end of the line said, "Now wait a minute, you're probably thinking of your last election; but think of all your successes and what you can do."

The depression started to lift and an idea came to Dottie. What if her breakout session was related to her loss for the Senate seat? It might help other people and prove cathartic for her. And that is what she did. Her session was titled "Reaching High, Falling Far, and Moving On." Dottie's session had more attendees than any other session, and the attendees loved it because they had all had similar experiences.

For Dottie, this session and its content evolved into a class on risk-taking that she taught at the University of Denver. Because of the encouragement and social support she received by being asked to speak at a conference, Dottie learned that she wasn't a failure after all.

Dottie Lamm

I Thought My Middle Name Was "Cabezudo" (Spanish for Stubborn) – *Christine Arguello*

Growing up as the oldest girl with four brothers and a sister, Christine Arguello was called "Christy Cabezudo" so many times by her mother that she thought "Cabezudo" (Spanish for stubborn or hardheaded) was her middle name. Expected to iron, clean the dishes, and do many household chores, Christy decided at a young age that she would not get married – she would not have a man telling her what to do! She also decided at a young age that she would graduate from high school, college, *and* go to Harvard Law School.

Life holds many surprises for all of us, and Christy was no exception. She did graduate from high school – a first generation high school graduate. She did get into college – the first generation in her family to go to college – at the University of Colorado at Boulder – where she met a man during her first week. He was a junior who also cooked and cleaned, and wasn't afraid of her intellect. They got married four months after they met, and they both graduated from college.

And then, as had been her dream for years, she applied to only one law school – Harvard. And she was accepted – the first generation in her family, again. She and her husband arrived in Cambridge, Massachusetts, sight unseen, and proceeded to experience total culture shock on every level. Christy says the support of her husband got her through the difficult times at Harvard, which included racial and gender discrimination – the latter, surprisingly, almost entirely from the Latino men at Harvard.

Christine Arguello

With the support of her husband, Christy continued pursuing her dream – her law career. When big law firms in Boston wouldn't hire all five foot one inch, ninety pounds of her as a potential trial lawyer, she and her husband moved to Miami where she worked for a smaller firm that did believe she could be a trial attorney.

Her husband supported her every step of the way – sacrificing his career for hers. He was the dominant parent at home, taking responsibility for their four children – before and after school – and doing the cooking and most of the cleaning. He also helped raise their two oldest granddaughters.

Christy did succeed in her career as an attorney and a judge. Her stubbornness, her determination to pursue her dream, and a supportive husband made it all possible.

CHAPTER 4

Moral Compass – Spirituality

The term **"moral compass"** means having a keen sense of right and wrong that functions as a needle to guide behavior – just like a needle on a compass. People with a moral compass have a core set of principles and strive to adhere to them. These principles guide their behavior and decision-making, resulting in increased ethical principles that in turn guide appropriate behavior. A person's moral compass may be accompanied by a sense of **spirituality**, but it may also stand alone. Many types of spirituality, or other-connectedness, can guide one's moral compass.

People with a moral compass do the right thing. They know what the right thing is, and they know to follow the golden rule. Even when no one is looking, people with a moral compass know that character counts in everything they do.

Spirituality means a connection with something higher than ourselves. This spirituality may or may not take the form of conventional, denominational religious beliefs. Spiritual people often manifest compassion, love for others, and selflessness.

Both their character and their belief systems guided these women through the obstacles in their lives.

Whatever Color They Turn Up, That's the Color I Take Them –
Dr. Justina Ford

Dr. Justina Ford battled discrimination on two fronts during her entire medical career: she was both a woman and African American. She herself didn't practice any discrimination. Her moral compass was strong. As Justina says it, "Folks make an appointment and I wait for them to come or go to see them; and whatever color they turn up, that's the color I take them."

Justina knew as a child that she was going to be a doctor. She loved to "play hospital" with her friends, but she would only play if she was the doctor! After medical school in Chicago in 1902, Justina moved to Denver. When she paid the money for her medical license, the state employee told her, "I feel dishonest taking a fee from you. You've got two strikes against you to begin with. First of all, you're a lady and second, you're colored."

Although she was not allowed to practice in any hospital in Denver for many years because of her race, she nevertheless built a healthy practice and a good reputation by making house calls, treating immigrants, visiting migrant camps, and delivering babies. Justina's careful attention to cleanliness was also well received and made the home births she attended safer than births in the hospital – which was crowded and unclean. In addition, she spoke eight languages – so that she would be able to communicate with almost any of her patients.

Justina developed a habit of spending an hour alone every evening. During that hour she read, wrote, studied, prayed, or meditated. People said her kindness and spirituality were revealed in her eyes.

As late as 1950, Justina was the only female African American doctor in Colorado. Belatedly, she was admitted to the Colorado Medical Society and thus by extension to the American Medical Association.

Justina, who "treated people no matter what color they showed up," dreamed of a time "when all

Dr. Justina Ford

the fears, hate, and even some death is over; and we will really be brothers, as God intended us to be in this land. This I believe. For this, I have worked my whole life."

If You're Right, You Don't Give Up –
Rachel B. Noel

Rachel B. Noel fought racial discrimination in its many forms all of her life. She said, "I have a deep faith that if you're right, you don't give up. And that's what I felt – that I was right, and somebody had to stand up."

Throughout her life, Rachel didn't give up, and she always stood up for what she believed. The granddaughter of a slave, she learned while growing up that education was very important. During her graduate work in education, equality in education became one of her very strong beliefs. Her focus became to work to strengthen educational opportunity for all children.

When she worked in Washington, D.C., one of Rachel's responsibilities was to serve as a leader of a Girl Scout troop. During that experience, she saw how poverty limited opportunities for some of the girls. As a result, she helped many Girl Scout parents raise money to buy the fabric that could be used for making the girls' uniforms.

After her family's move to Denver, Rachel learned that the Denver Public School system was, actually, de facto segregated. Even though by law there was to be equality throughout the school system, the truth was that the schools were segregated by neighborhood, and that meant they were definitely not equal. Black students were sent to the inferior schools in their neighborhoods, while white students went to observably better schools in their separate neighborhoods. Because housing was essentially segregated, their neighborhood schools were as well.

Rachel B. Noel

Standing up for "what was right," Rachel ran for election to the Denver Public School Board and became the first African American woman to be elected to public office in Colorado. She was also the first Black person to be elected to the Denver Public School Board. While on the board, Rachel worked tirelessly for desegregation of the schools – always standing up for what she knew was right.

Her advocacy for equal education and opportunity for all students continued throughout her life. She became a prominent civil rights leader and an articulate spokesperson for equal opportunity in education. She accumulated many more firsts and awards for her beliefs and accomplishments, including a stained glass window of her likeness in the Colorado State Capitol. Rachel knew what was right. She didn't give up. Her moral compass was strong. And she chose to always stand up for what she believed.

Bringing Joy to the World Through Dance –
Cleo Parker Robinson

For Cleo Parker Robinson, a near-death experience when she was ten years old has informed every decision she has since made in her life. She believes that we each have to have a will to live. In addition, her agreement with her Creator was that "her life would be in movement."

At age ten, Cleo came down with a kidney infection. Her kidneys shut down, leading to rheumatic fever and a heart attack. Cleo's mother was Caucasian and her father was African American. Because she was in Dallas, Texas, with segregated hospitals, the ambulance driver couldn't figure out which hospital to take her to. If she went to the Black hospital, her white mother couldn't come with her. But, because she had one Black parent, she was considered Black and therefore couldn't go to the white hospital. This presented an impossible dilemma.

The delay resulted in a near-death experience for Cleo, with her Black grandparents literally "praying her back to life." Every day after that was "a party" for her – every day, "she was going to dance with her brothers and sisters!" But, after finding out that dancing was not allowed in the Methodist church she attended, she decided to create her own church, her own spiritual home, complete with dancing. At age twelve, Cleo choreographed her first piece, "To My Father's House," and she hasn't stopped dancing since. Cleo says that she danced that very first piece all the way around the world, including dancing it with Dr. Martin Luther King, Jr. and Bishop Desmond Tutu.

Cleo started teaching dance when she was sixteen years old, and she hasn't stopped that either. She says her soul understood that she needed to bring people together through music

Cleo Parker Robinson

and dance. Her motto, "One spirit, many voices," resonates throughout her life. She brings people together in their highest selves with a language that has no barriers. Cleo brings joy to the world through dance!

Be Proud of Who We Are –
Sister Alicia Cuarón

Sister Alicia Cuarón says that the messages she learned from her family – "be proud of who we are and of our culture, our history, and our heritage" – enabled her to face the systemic racism against Latinos, particularly women, she has encountered throughout her life. She also learned from her family how to "move on" and "to do the best that she could do." She encapsulates the lessons she learned in what she calls "the three P's – pride, passion, and personal power."

Sister Alicia particularly emphasizes that consistently, people didn't think she was very smart. As a result, she did not hesitate to pull out her credentials, specifically her PhD, when the occasion demanded it. She then proved her capabilities and demonstrated she could handle the situations that came her way. In addition, once she became aware of the frequency with which she was given the table in the restaurant next to the bathroom or the hotel room next to the elevator, she advocated for herself and refused the poorly placed table and demanded to be changed to another, more desirable room.

Sister Alicia counsels others to take pride in "who you are, your traditions, your culture, your history, the language you speak at home, your values and your community." She says that one has to have a passion to really go after something. At first, for her, that something was the American dream. But once she had achieved her own American dream, she realized something else was the answer for her. That something else became a decision to pivot to enter religious life and focus her efforts on the poor, the marginalized, immigrants – all for the common good. With her focus on spirituality and passion, she describes her personal power – feeling both strong and good about herself.

Sister Alicia Cuarón

Understanding where she came from, as well as being proud of her culture and "who we are," provided a strong foundation for Sister Alicia and empowered her to take the next step during every phase of her life.

I Respond with Kindness –
Sister Lydia Peña

Sister Lydia Peña recalls the closing of Loretto Heights College in 1988 as very painful. In addition to the sadness she felt about the closing itself, many of her colleagues in the Order of Loretto regarded her as a traitor when she accepted an offer to go to Regis University to teach. Yet she says she always tries to respond to such challenges with kindness, a spiritual reaction, which she describes as "a faith-filled, hope-filled, love-filled response."

When she was three years old, Sister Lydia developed a severe case of double pneumonia. The doctor said she would not live through the night. However, her Aunt Rosita wrapped her in an herbal blanket – chamomile, tea, sage, and indigenous herbs, including lavender. By the morning, Lydia had sweated out her fever and was crying. Since then, she has lived a long and healthy life.

When Lydia decided to enter the Sisters of Loretto Order, her mother said they needed to go visit and thank Aunt Rosita, and they did. Aunt Rosita said to Sister Lydia, "Remember it was your Protestant aunt who saved you!"

This early obstacle and the person who saved her life taught Sister Lydia to value people regardless of who they were or to which culture, gender, or religious tradition they belonged. Such identifying but superficial characteristics should not determine whether individuals had value.

Sister Lydia says she has learned that her response to any situation is up to her, and that nobody else can respond for her. She says she is "in charge of her life," and she knows that very clearly. Whether or not people value what she has done, she believes it is up to her to respond with kindness. She wants to treat other people well, regardless of whether they reciprocate.

Sister Lydia Peña

Sister Lydia believes that she is here on Earth to benefit "the other" – and to be useful. She also understands that the obstacles we encounter in life often present new "growing and learning opportunities." And, she tries, as much as she can, to always respond to whatever situation she is presented with – with kindness.

Doing the Right Things for Kids –
Shari Shink

Shari Shink's north star is doing the right things for abused, neglected, and foster children. She believes that if she is fearless and has the courage to do what others are not willing or able to do, she can step in and make something happen. And she believes that foster, abused, and neglected children have gifts, and that those gifts should be fully developed and utilized.

Shari's beliefs were sorely tested shortly after she moved to Colorado. After establishing what today is the Rocky Mountain Children's Law Center, she and the center were precluded from representing the cases of children in the Denver juvenile court system. She says she was immobilized for about a millisecond by the ban.

Since Shari knew the right things needed to be done for kids in Denver and throughout Colorado, she was committed to find ways around, over, under, or through the ban. And, that is what she did. The Rocky Mountain Children's Law Center then expanded its reach to kids from around the entire state of Colorado. But to reach kids in Denver, Shari approached one of the biggest law firms in town and asked them to represent kids in the Denver court, pro bono. Denver kids who needed support would then be represented by outstanding legal professionals in court. Although the ban lasted for ten years, she was successful in doing the right things for kids.

Shari believes that all children should have a chance to thrive in the world and develop their talents to the fullest. Sometimes, parents don't have the skills or wherewithal to nurture their children in any way. She "can't stand it" when she knows that kids are abused or neglected, and she feels compelled to intervene and make a difference in their lives.

Shari Shink

With her moral compass, Shari has worked for her entire career to "do the right things" for kids.

CHAPTER 5

Determination – Perseverance – Persistence

Although not quite identical, the three concepts of **determination**, **perseverance**, and **persistence** are closely related. Because they are almost synonymous, they are often used interchangeably. All three terms imply a "stick-to-it-ive-ness" in the face of opposition or difficulty.

Determination means the firmness of purpose or resoluteness on the way to achieving one's goal. Determined people keep going and don't take no for an answer. They forge past the naysayers, doubters, and skeptics, unwavering on their path. They don't let "no one has ever done that before" stop them. And especially, they don't let "you can't do that" or "women can't do that" stop them.

Persistence means that one keeps on doing something – pursuing a course of action – in spite of difficulties or opposition, or in spite of the fact that the task is hard. It also means keeping on doing something in spite of not succeeding the first time. Or the fifth time. Or the hundredth time. Or, in the case of Thomas Edison and the incandescent light bulb, not succeeding until more than one thousand experiments had been conducted. It is the capacity to not give up.

Perseverance means persisting in doing something even though success has yet to have been achieved and in spite of the fact that difficulties may be encountered along the way. The person with perseverance believes that the solution will be found, it just hasn't been discovered yet. They believe that each step is a step toward the resolution. These women felt there was no turning back. No giving up. They would be successful. They would find a way.

🏆 🏆 🏆

God Forbid I Should Go to Any Heaven Where There Are No Horses –
Anna Lee Aldred

Anna Lee Aldred started riding horses shortly after she began to walk. She won her first race at six years old. She lived and loved horses. She even said, "God forbid I should go to any heaven where there are no horses." But getting her license as a jockey so she could race horses – not so easy.

As a teenager, Anna Lee was racing horses all over Colorado and Wyoming. When she was approaching adulthood and wanted to get her license as a jockey, no racetrack in the United States would issue her one. Being very determined and not one to take no for an answer, she went to Tijuana, Mexico, and applied for her jockey's license at the Agua Caliente Racetrack. Track officials there really didn't want to license her either but could find no rule prohibiting women from becoming professional jockeys. So, they granted her a license. That was 1939.

Anna Lee lost her first race by a nose, but she won many races at county and state fairs over the next few years. Then she came up against an obstacle she couldn't overcome. She had grown from less than 100 pounds when she was 18 in 1939, to 5 feet 5 inches tall and 118 pounds. That was too tall and too heavy for a jockey.

Anna Lee Aldred

Not one to be deterred from her love of horses, however, she taught herself to be a trick rider on the rodeo circuit. Her tricks included standing on the saddle of a horse and hanging off the side by one foot. Although she retired from the rodeo circuit after her marriage, she rode a horse almost every day for the next thirty-five years as she worked on the family cattle ranch. After her divorce, she helped move horses around before races.

In her last years, she even slept under a horse blanket. Anna Lee was hopeful that when she was gone she would be sent to a "heaven with horses."

I Just Hope They Think I Did More Good Than Harm –
Lena Archuleta

The first Latina principal in the Denver Public Schools, Lena Archuleta grew up being taught that getting an education was of prime importance. As a child, she "played school" all summer – always serving as the teacher. Not only did she strive for excellence in all her educational and other endeavors, she was known and recognized throughout the community for encouraging others to do the same. She worked to improve life for all people – definitely doing "more good than harm" during her lifetime.

Although raised in an impoverished family in New Mexico, Lena was able to pursue a college education on scholarship. She then embarked on what would be a thirty-year career in education. At a time when Latino students were walking out of schools to protest the lack of attention and respect, Lena was climbing the administrative ladder at the Denver Public Schools.

Her commitment to ensuring that every student was able to have an education led to her work with bilingual education. In the beginning of bilingual education, students who were Spanish speaking were taught English, and those who were English speaking were taught Spanish. Lena also worked with a broad range of Latino-serving nonprofit organizations to help students complete their education, including being able to attend college.

And Lena never stopped getting an education herself. She earned a master's degree in library science and then returned to get a certificate in school administration. The latter facilitated her appointment as principal.

Lena demonstrated her perseverance in her articulation of her life philosophy: "You just don't quit. Just stick in there and put one foot ahead of the other, and just

Lena Archuleta

work with it and do your best." She also said, "I think there's always going to be somebody who's going to be standing behind you and help you if you get in trouble."

Lena was certainly there for others, serving as an inspiration in all she did. She definitely is remembered for "doing more good than harm."

And Yet She Persisted –
Emily Howell Warner

Emily Howell Warner fell in love with flying when she took her first flight. That was in the 1950s. When she visited the cockpit, she loved the view, as well as the dials and switches. One of the pilots suggested that she take flying lessons. When she found out that girls could learn to fly, she was ecstatic.

Flight lessons were expensive – her weekly salary was $38.00 and the lessons were $12.75 per hour. Yet she persisted. By the time she was eighteen, she had her student pilot's license. By twenty-one, she had her private pilot's license and took every opportunity to get more flying hours. She earned every rating she could – including commercial, instrument, multiengine, and instructor.

In 1960, she became a flight instructor, and in 1967, she became a Federal Aviation Administration examiner. As she tested the pilots, she realized that she could be – like them – an airline pilot. And in 1968, she began applying to the commercial airlines for jobs as a pilot. For five years, she applied without success to multiple airlines, multiple times. Even though she did not get a positive response to any of her applications, she persisted.

In 1973, she heard that Frontier Airlines had just announced its new class of hires – and her name was not on the list. Being the determined person she was, she went to the Frontier Airlines office and got an interview. Although no one else who had applied for a pilot's job had to take a check flight on a simulator, Emily was required to do so – on one of the toughest airplanes around.

Emily knew she had succeeded when the man interviewing her lamented that the pilot's uniform didn't come in women's sizes! When she was hired in 1973, Emily had more than seven thousand hours in her logbook – more

Emily Howell Warner

than four times the minimum number required to be an airline pilot. She was the first woman hired by a commercial airline as a pilot. Emily made her first flight as a copilot in 1974, and she became the first female captain in an American commercial airline company in 1976.

Today, Emily Howell Warner's Frontier Airline pilot's uniform hangs in the Smithsonian National Air and Space Museum in Washington, D.C. All because she persisted!

Because I Didn't Get into Yale –
Pat Schroeder

Pat Schroeder's introduction to Harvard Law School in 1961 did not begin auspiciously. The men in the class kept saying to her and the thirteen other women, "Don't you realize you're taking a position from a man?"

Then the dean invited the fourteen women to his home for dinner. Pat was grateful for the opportunity to meet him. He was not welcoming, however, and the food was terrible. In fact, he kept telling them that he did not approve of having women at the school. He said they had to build a wom-

Pat Schroeder

en's restroom, which was taking money away from the library. Although he had protested the restroom, he had gotten overruled by the board.

After dinner, he had the women sit in their folding chairs in a circle and he asked them to tell him why they came to Harvard Law School. For Pat, the nightmare was continuing. But her classmate from California, Ann Dudley Cronkite, looked the dean squarely in the eye and said, "I'm here because I didn't get into

Yale!" He lost his composure, and Pat learned an important lesson that evening on how to deal with bullies.

Pat says this incident laid the foundation for her twenty-four years in the US Congress. Whenever she had a difficult situation to deal with, her determination came to her aid as she remembered Ann Dudley Cronkite's retort, "Because I didn't get into Yale!"

Moving Mountains –
Maria Guajardo

As dean of the faculty of international liberal arts at Soka University, a private university in Tokyo, Japan, Maria Guajardo has had to "move mountains" in order to achieve her goals. She was recruited to be the first female dean and the first non-Japanese dean at the university. All of the classes in her newly formed department, where she was the first dean, would be taught in English. This was another first for the university. Her job included recruiting faculty from around the world, developing new admissions practices, developing curricula, and recruiting Japanese students who spoke English as well as international students. The mountains were pretty big.

As she pursued these complex tasks, everything Maria knew about leadership was challenged, both because she was a woman and because she realized that her view of leadership was very Western, especially compared to the Asian environment in which she was operating. But she also came to the conclusion that she needed to take action and contribute in a way that reflected her knowledge base and skill set. Within thirty days of her arrival, she drafted a proposal, which she presented to the university president: she would offer a Women's Leadership Initiative for faculty, staff, and students. The president said yes, but the faculty and staff were quite resistant.

"Why do you want to train women?" she was asked. "They'll just get married; they don't need to be trained." When she requested to reserve a room to hold her training in, she was told no rooms were available. She decided, then, that they could meet in the hallway, outside, or in her office. That mountain wasn't going to stand in her way.

For training international staff, she was told that, yes, she could offer six weeks of a leadership workshop, but not during office hours – another mountain around which she figured out a way. Although

Maria Guajardo

some of her colleagues didn't appreciate that she'd been moving mountains, Maria's classes continue to be oversubscribed, and she has to turn away 60 to 70 percent of the students who apply.

Maria believes that being the children of immigrants helped her figure out how to move those mountains. When they came to this country from Mexico, her parents were illiterate and didn't know English. They didn't know how to navigate the system. They didn't know how to negotiate. But Maria learned all of those skills, and she applied them when she later arrived in Japan, a country that can be very discriminatory toward foreigners. Maria now feels great empathy toward her parents and understands more than she ever did about how they felt when they came to the United States.

When asked how she feels now about all those mountains she has had to move? She responds proudly, "I have no regrets. I wouldn't have missed this opportunity for anything." Maria personifies persistence.

I Learned to Stand My Ground –
LaRae Orullian

LaRae Orullian learned a lesson early in her life: when she stood her ground, things usually turned out better for her.

That lesson was learned when she was five or six years old. The school bully picked on her regularly, and she often came home from school crying. One day, her mother asked her why she let him pick on her. LaRae said she didn't know how to stop him, so her mother gave her permission to poke him in the nose the next time he bothered her. And LaRae did poke him in the nose. He never bothered her again, and LaRae found a freedom that she had not had before.

LaRae not only got permission from her mother to poke a bully in the nose, she was also encouraged by her mother to do whatever she wanted to do – as long as it was within the law and within the honor code of conduct. LaRae learned from this experience to always seek opportunity – even if the experience is not successful, it provides a chance for learning.

The freedom that LaRae found and the opportunities she pursued would prove important, later, for her banking career. After many years at a bank in Denver, she was named to be an officer – the first woman at the bank to be promoted to an officer level. All of the men who had made officer were sent to graduate banking school, and LaRae wanted to go too. The bank officials said, "No! No, you're a woman. You can't go."

LaRae did not let that stop her. She applied to The Ohio State Graduate Banking School and received a scholarship from the National Association of Bank Women. Then she went to the president of the bank and asked for the time off to attend school. Again, she was told, "No." For three years, she took her own vacation time to attend the Graduate Banking School in Ohio. She knew she needed the training, just as the men needed it. She was determined and found a way.

LaRae Orullian

And that training paid off. When the Women's Bank was established in Colorado, LaRae was asked to be its inaugural president. After much indecision on her part, she realized that just as she had spent her life teaching other women to move up in banking – she herself now had the opportunity of a lifetime. She put aside her fears and took that challenging opportunity.

Now, women whom she meets in the community frequently thank her for being the leader of the only bank that would loan them money for their new business or to buy a home for themselves.

LaRae's example of "standing her ground" and "always pursuing opportunities" enabled many other women to pursue *their* very own dreams. LaRae has been a real inspiration for countless other women.

We Don't Need Any More Women in Ag –
Diana Wall

Diana Wall was stunned very early in her academic career when a full professor said, upon meeting her in the halls of the institution where she was teaching on a temporary assignment, "Oh you're that girl in ag? We don't need any more women in ag."

Although she was aware there weren't very many women in plant pathology, her area at the time, she hadn't before personally experienced the gender discrimination that was now directed at her. Diana says that she was saddened "almost to despair" for about twenty-four hours. And then she put her head down and said the equivalent of, "I'll show you. You don't know me. You weren't in my class. I got the best teacher award at the school. I'm now going to be aware of this type of behavior. And I'm going to see how I can survive in this field." And survive she did. In fact, she thrived.

Diana grew up in a household where her mother particularly wanted her to have a broad range of experiences. Diana took ballet lessons; played the clarinet; learned French, Spanish, and Latin; and, later, took art history (for which she earned a grade of D). The rule was that if she failed, she had to do it again. That philosophy instilled a strong sense of determination in Diana.

She characterizes her outlook as "expecting that there will be hurdles in life." She recommends building a support network.

"Get lots of colleagues and friends who you can call on to help you when you run into these hurdles," she says. "Call on people who have run into these hurdles before and can guide you with their reactions and experiences," she adds. "And, do not take it personally if things go wrong." Diana concludes, "If the opportunity that came your way is really a bad one – then leave it. If you want to stay and fight, please

Diana Wall

do so. But if that is not your choice, other opportunities will come your way."

And they did come Diana's way. Today, she is a world-renowned ecologist and has spent more than twenty-five years in Antarctica studying soil diversity and invertebrate communities. The Wall Valley in Antarctica and a soil microarthropod species are named for her. And all because she was determined and didn't let someone saying, "We don't need another woman in ag" stand in her way.

CHAPTER 6

Optimism

Optimism is a mindset that enables people to view the world, other people, and events in a generally favorable and positive light. Optimistic people have confidence that things will turn out well in the future. They believe if they work hard, they will succeed. The successful optimists see life's problems and are able to incorporate them into their thought processes as they proceed through their lives. They tend to focus on positive outcomes and problems that can be solved, and they learn to move on or reframe difficulties. As Winston Churchill said, "An optimist sees the opportunity in every difficulty."

Optimistic people believe they will figure something out. And, if they don't, someone will help them. They will find a way that will show them how to solve the problem with which they are faced. Inspiration will come, leading them to a solution. Optimistic people don't say, "I can't." They say, "I will do it." They say, "I can do it." They are the personification of the small engine in the *Little Engine That Could* that pulled the long train up the mountain while repeating, "I think I can. I think I can." And optimistic people think, after arriving at a solution, "I thought I could. I thought I could," which reinforces their can-do spirit.

These women never said, "I can't." They believed they could find the opportunity in the difficulty – and they did.

I Give Hope – That Is What I Do! –
Marilyn Van Derbur Atler

When incest survivor and former Miss America Marilyn Van Derbur Atler was in recovery, she wanted to meet one woman – just one woman – who had made it through recovery and went on to live her life. When she realized that she herself was going to recover, she knew she would go back on speaking tours to help others through their shame. Her message is, "If I can get through this, you can do it, too!" Marilyn's optimism gives incest survivors hope.

Marilyn Van Derbur Atler survived incest that began when she was five years old and continued until she was eighteen. She did not pursue beauty pageants. In fact, she was out of the room when her sorority sisters at the University of Colorado at Boulder elected her as their candidate for Miss Colorado. After she won the Miss Colorado competition, she went on to win the Miss America pageant, becoming Miss America in 1958.

Being Miss America provided her with a platform from which to serve as a beacon of hope to other incest survivors. Whenever she speaks, the first thing she does is ask all survivors in the room to stand. This is a necessary first step to aid in their recovery. Her experience is that many people in the room are so overcome with shame that they cannot stand. They think they are "dirty" and that once their secret is revealed, no one will speak to them, and their life as they know it will crumble. But when they stand, they discover that their life is not over; people still like them. In the words of Marilyn's daughter, Jennifer, "Why are you ashamed, Mommy? You didn't do anything wrong."

From being chosen to be on the cover of *People* magazine to the publication of her own book, *Miss America by Day*, to being the subject of documentaries, Marilyn strives to help people overcome their shame. She believes her

Marilyn Van Derbur Atler

role is to be the woman she herself wanted to find when she was in recovery. With her extraordinary smile, she now says, emphatically: "I give hope – that is what I do!"

The Only Thing I Had Control Over
Was My Attitude –
Penny Hamilton

Penny Hamilton learned early in life that the only thing she could control was her attitude – and she was determined, as she moved through her life, to succeed. And Penny says, "Failure is okay, too, as long as you learn from that, but it should still be avoided, if at all possible."

Penny grew up in a household with an alcoholic father who often beat her mother. As a result, Penny says she learned to adapt to various situations and she learned to "read" people. She said that she also read continuously, and she learned about many successful people who had come from dysfunctional backgrounds like hers – so she knew she could overcome the chaos too.

Penny attended Catholic school where she reveled in the structure – a complete counterpoint to the chaos at home. She believed her ticket out of the chaos was higher education, and she knew she would have to get scholarships to go to college – which she did. She also says that like her father, she too has an addictive personality – and her addiction is work.

Penny is a two-time survivor of breast cancer – in 2007 and 2015. Her optimistic attitude shines radiantly when she discusses the treatment, especially comparing the differences that had transpired between the first occurrence and the second, as well as her worldwide support system. Her positive attitude is also evident when she talks about her reaction to her treatment. She visualized that the radiation was a laser, which blasted all of the remaining cancer cells out of her body. She thinks of the pills that she takes as power pills that are surging through her body.

Penny Hamilton

Penny says many people around the world have life-threatening problems. She believes that you can always find a situation that is worse than yours, so "just keep your eyes focused ahead and keep going."

Penny focuses on the future and not the disease. The dashboard of her car has pictures of her in an airplane and pictures of her new book cover.

Penny learned early in her life that the only thing she had control over was her attitude. She believed she would be successful, that she would overcome obstacles, and that she would achieve her goals. And she did.

Better to Light One Little Candle
Than to Curse the Darkness –
Martha Urioste

Martha Urioste says that during her forty-five-year career in the Denver Public Schools, any time there was a major problem to address, it seemed someone would ask her to fix it. Actually, she says, they would just assign her the problem to fix. But with her relentless optimism and her belief that it is "better to light one little candle than to curse the darkness," Martha would rise to the occasion and handle the problem.

The specific problem that enabled Martha to find her passion was being assigned to one of the high schools in Denver. The task was to address the school dropout problem. When Martha inadvertently discovered Montessori education, she "fell in love" with the idea that Montessori could really help children so they wouldn't drop out of school. Helping young children – three, four, and five years old – learn to love learning was possible through Montessori, she believed. Then they would be set for a lifelong love of learning and would not drop out of school.

Martha asked to be sent, as the principal, to an elementary school with the intention of implementing a Montessori program. She was then assigned to the toughest school in Northeast Denver, in which only 18 percent of the children were meeting the district's educational standards. The children were poor, and the community was blighted. In addition, the school was out of compliance with the desegregation order from the US District Court.

Martha Urioste

After nine years of Martha's leadership and the implementation of Montessori education, 50 percent of the students were meeting educational standards, the school was second in the city in terms of academic scores, and the community and parents had coalesced around Martha's leadership.

This was not the end of the problems that Martha addressed during her career in the Denver Public Schools, but she had found her true north star – Montessori education. She has continued her Montessori education advocacy even after retirement. She has extended Montessori to very young children and to children in Uganda.

All of this occurred because Martha believed it was "better to light one little candle than to curse the darkness."

When One Door Closes,
Another One Opens –
Dorothy Horrell

Dorothy Horrell thought that becoming president of the Colorado Community College System was going to be the final stop along her career path. But it wasn't. Almost as soon as she retired from that position, she found that another opportunity came her way – one door had closed but another one had opened.

Growing up in a large family and being the granddaughter of immigrant grandparents, Dorothy says, "You didn't wallow in your troubles because there just wasn't time to do so. If something isn't going the way you want it to, or isn't getting done the way it needs to get done, you just step up and you do it! You just figure it out and you don't feel sorry for yourself." In addition, Dorothy came out of her childhood with an optimistic attitude convinced that she was "going to bend, but not break."

Dorothy was the first woman to be tapped for the presidency of the Colorado Community College System when she was only forty-seven years old. Two and a half years later, she retired. Almost immediately thereafter, she heard about a job opening at the Bonfils-Stanton Foundation. Dorothy had never worked in philanthropy or the nonprofit world – she had been in academia for her entire career – but she applied for the position, was selected, and became the president and CEO of the foundation. Another door had opened.

Dorothy retired again in 2013. But another door opened, and in 2016 she became the chancellor of the University of Colorado at Denver.

Dorothy says that we are all products of where we've come from and the experiences that we've had. She even has a saying, "No experience we've ever had is wasted." And, what she means is that any experience, whether it is an exhilarating and positive experi-

Dorothy Horrell

ence or a challenging one, is a learning experience. She says, "You'll always learn something, if you are paying attention."

Dorothy has learned that hard work and competence are important but are not always sufficient to get you where you want to go. And, she has learned that keeping one's eyes open is really important. "That's the only way you'll see that another door has opened, after the previous one has closed," she said.

I Bloom Where I Was Planted –
Carol Mutter

Carol Mutter didn't expect to be the first female two-star and three-star general in the US Marine Corps, but she took advantage of opportunities presented to her and learned how to "bloom where she was planted."

Growing up poor in a small rural Colorado town, Carol had forty-two students in her high school graduating class. Although her mother had graduated from high school but her father had not, they expected Carol and her brother to both graduate from high school and go to college.

The only way Carol could afford to go to college was to live at home. She attended the local college, which today is called the University of Northern Colorado, and she planned to become a high school math teacher. Then, a letter from a marine corps recruiter was sent to all junior and senior women students at her college. The letter told about an opportunity that the marine corps was offering. Her mother threw the letter away – but Carol happened to go through the student union on the way to class and spoke with the marine corps recruiter. She says that "the rest is history."

Joining the marine corps was never in Carol's long-range plan. But the requirement was a three-year commitment, and she figured she could return to teaching when her marine corps career was completed. However, Carol "bloomed where she was planted."

She met her husband in the marine corps and credits him with helping her become more assertive. Although Carol believes that the top level school (graduate education provided by a branch of the military that prepares senior officers and civilians for executive leadership assignments) she attended wasn't the right one, networking with fellow attendees proved career determining. After her husband's son was

Carol Mutter

diagnosed with leukemia and her husband was assigned to Colorado to be near him, one of her former top level school classmates advocated for her to also be assigned to Colorado. And she was in the right place at the right time when the law was changed. That change allowed women to be promoted to the rank of admiral in the navy or general in the army and marine corps. She says, with humor, "They saw me coming, so they changed the law!"

Carol says she lives by Romans 8:38 in her Christian Bible, and she quoted, "All things work together for good."

As she ascended the ranks in the marine corps, Carol displayed her optimistic attitude to work together with others and "bloomed where she was planted."

CHAPTER 7

Creativity

Creativity is the ability to be imaginative or inventive. The creative person takes traditional ideas, rules, patterns, or relationships and creates new ideas, rules, patterns, or relationships. Although creativity is often thought to apply mainly to artists and entertainers, every type of problem solving generally benefits from creative thought.

Creative people take risks. They are very curious. Often, they are not content with the "way we've always done it." They willingly or out of necessity try new ways of doing things. They are not afraid to look foolish. And they realize that it is okay, maybe even important, to have fun in life.

Creativity has no bounds. As Maya Angelou said, "You can't use up creativity. The more you use, the more you have." The women in this chapter found new ways – creative ways – to live their lives and face obstacles.

Woman's Work –
Martha Maxwell

Taxidermist Martha Maxwell was frustrated by the incredulous questions signifying doubt that a woman could have prepared the specimens and habitats at her wildlife displays at the 1876 Centennial Exposition in Philadelphia. So she put up a sign that read, "Woman's Work."

Martha had experienced many of the other duties commonly associated with "women's work" during her lifetime. Years before, after marrying James Maxwell, a widower with four children, and settling in Wisconsin, her time was consumed with cooking, cleaning, and child care. Yet the lessons she had learned as a youngster about animals and birds from her grandmother Abigail stayed with her. Since she had come from a line of independent women, as she could she got involved in the reform movements of the day – women's suffrage, abolition, and temperance.

After the financial crash of 1857, Martha's husband, James, decided to seek his fortune in gold in Colorado, and Martha willingly went with him. After the boardinghouse they ran burned down, they returned to their squatter's cabin, only to find it occupied. One of the occupants was a taxidermist, and Martha was fascinated with his specimens, as well as with his materials and tools. She set her mind on becoming a taxidermist.

Life and "women's work" inter-
vened again, but eventually Martha
made it to Boulder, Colorado, and
was able to pursue her dream. She
had to learn how to handle a gun.
She had to learn how to clean and
prepare animals. She hiked for
hours to observe animals in their
natural habitats. She used her creativity to develop new techniques to
make large animals appear beautiful and realistic. In addition, her

Martha Maxwell

exhibits showed the animals in displays that resembled their natural habitats.

By 1868, Martha had six hundred specimens and had displayed them at the Third Annual Exposition of the Colorado
Agricultural Society. At the governor's behest, she represented
Colorado at the St. Louis Fair in 1870. By 1874, she had her own
museum, and she displayed her specimens at the Centennial Exposition in Philadelphia in 1876.

Martha was not deterred by the comments she heard in Philadelphia, for she said, "My life is one of physical work, an effort
to prove the words spoken by more gifted women. . . . The world
demands proof of woman's capacities, without it, words are useless."
Martha Maxwell truly did "Woman's Work."

Elitch Gardens, the "Picture I Painted for All to Enjoy" –
Mary Elitch Long

Mary Elitch Long loved her gardens and her animals. The experience she created for others – Elitch Gardens, the world-renowned Denver gardens and amusement park – brought her a great deal of joy. She said, "I have never spent a summer away from the Gardens, the 'picture I painted for all to enjoy.' Every tree holds it owns story for me; every flower its own memory." The people of Denver and Colorado – and the world over – have benefited from her creativity.

Mary Elitch's zest for life was severely tested after her husband, John, died of pneumonia when she was only thirty-four – less than a year after Elitch Zoological Gardens had opened. After crying and crying, Mary looked around the gardens, fixed up some empty and broken flower pots, and decided to reopen the gardens after it had been closed for the season. Hers was the only zoo between Chicago and the West Coast, and it was the only zoo in the world to be owned by a woman.

When Mary had financial difficulties, she sold stock to investors. But the attractions she offered from the opening in 1890 – the animals, the gardens, band concerts, a miniature railroad, and a steam calliope – brought many customers, and she was able to buy the stock back. Over the years, she added opera, plays – including the oldest summer stock repertory theater in the country – symphony orchestras, brass bands, and dance bands, as well as all of the usual family-oriented amusement park amenities.

Mary was always photographed with flowers. She wanted to have fun and she believed other people wanted excitement and entertainment too. Through her efforts, Elitch Gardens, which remains vibrant and attractive even today, became the "picture she painted for all to enjoy."

Mary Elitch Long

She Who Laughs . . . Lasts –
Josie Heath

When Josie Heath chaired the Board of County Commissioners in Boulder County, the board needed to rezone in accordance with the Boulder County Comprehensive Plan. Although the plan had been approved, the previous commissioners had not put in place the zoning to match it. As Josie relates it, not everyone was pleased with the rezoning, and a small group of very angry people appeared at the public meetings.

At one meeting, an old rancher came up to her holding a rope with a noose on it and said, "String her up." In addition, a recall effort was initiated to recall her as well as one of the other commissioners.

A woman was heading up the recall effort, and every week she reported on how easy it was to get signatures to support the recall. Big headlines were in the local paper regularly: HAVE YOU SIGNED A PETITION TO RECALL BOULDER COUNTY COMMISSIONERS HEATH AND STEWART?

Josie relates that she was "feeling lower than a snake's belly." Although it wasn't an election year, it was October, and Halloween was fast approaching. Halloween used to be a really big event on Boulder's Pearl Street pedestrian mall. Then, Josie got creative.

She would dress up for Halloween as her recall nemesis and gather signatures! Her nemesis was a woman who always wore her "Recall Heath" shirt, had a big bouffant hairstyle, had very long eyelashes, and wore a little red miniskirt. One of Josie's friends was able to get her one of the "Recall Heath" shirts – so she was ready. Josie had stewed about this situation for months and had decided, "Well, I'll just have a little fun with it. And I did!"

On Halloween, Josie put on a Dolly Parton wig, big fancy black eyelashes, a red miniskirt, and her "Recall Heath" shirt, and off to the mall she went. Although concerned that she would have signatures that she would have to deliver to the Recall

Josie Heath

Committee, the evening turned out better than she could have ever planned. People said, "Oh, I would never sign that petition, I think Josie Heath is doing a great job!"

The icing on the cake occurred about a week later. During a board meeting, the secretary slipped Josie a note that said the sheriff was on the phone – Josie thought she was going to get in trouble for impersonating someone on Halloween. No. The woman who was the head of the Recall Committee had called the sheriff's office to report a break-in at her house. All of the recall petitions with signatures had been stolen. But officers who were sent to the house found no sign of an intrusion, and nothing else was taken. The bottom line was that the head of the Recall Committee hadn't been able to get enough signatures to actually recall the two commissioners.

Josie thought, "Thank goodness," and was so glad she had decided to be brave and have a little fun with a situation that had caused her so much anguish for months. In the end, she found out that "she who laughs . . . lasts!"

CHAPTER 8

Resilience

Resilience in the physical sciences means "the ability to return to an original form after being bent or stretched." Resilience, when applied to people, is not that different in concept. People are deemed to be resilient if they adapt to difficult situations, find healthy ways to handle adversity, and recover well from addressing problems and confronting issues. Resilient people learn and grow from the adversities and challenges they have faced and addressed.

Resilient people understand – or have learned – that they will face setbacks throughout their lives. They become discouraged, but usually not for very long – one inductee said a millisecond, another said twenty-four hours. They are like the tree in the country and western song "Strong Enough to Bend":

> *There's a tree*
> *Out in the backyard*
> *That never has been broken by the wind*
> *And the reason it's still standing*
> *It was strong enough to bend.*

Resilient people learn – they learn how to handle problems and learn that neither the bad times nor the good times last forever.

They see situations as learning opportunities, try to figure out the lesson that situation is teaching them, and then apply the lesson. The women whose stories are told here didn't give up, and they were strong enough to bend.

Never Give Up! – *Clara Brown*

Former slave Clara Brown never gave up hope that she would find her daughter, who had been sold. Although it would take forty-seven years, she doggedly pursued every lead she could find, and her resilience paid off – she was successful.

Clara was born in Virginia as a slave. One of her four children drowned at age eight. She, her husband, and the remaining children were then sold when she was thirty-five – all to separate owners. Clara went to Kentucky, where she was granted her freedom at age fifty-six. She learned that her husband and daughter were dead and that the trail for her son was lost. But she was still determined to find her remaining daughter, Eliza Jane. What if that daughter had gone west? Clara herself was now in Kansas.

She offered her cooking services to a wagon train and arrived in Denver, Colorado, in 1859. She hired on at a bakery and helped found a Sunday School. Later, she moved to Gilpin County and opened a laundry, while serving as a cook and midwife. Clara saved her money and continued to look for her daughter. She was generous with her contributions and earned the affection of the townspeople who called her Aunt Clara.

Clara Brown

In 1866, she returned to Kentucky hoping to find Eliza Jane. Although that search was unsuccessful, Clara brought sixteen of her relatives and friends with her back to Colorado. In 1882, she received word that her daughter was in Council Bluffs, Iowa. Clara was now eighty-two years old and frail, but through the help of friends and her church, she managed to buy a train ticket to get to Iowa. It was with great joy that she did find her daughter in Council Bluffs.

Clara also met her granddaughter for the first time. Eliza Jane and Clara's granddaughter came to Denver to care for Clara. All this happened because Clara was resilient and never gave up!

Work Hard and Be the Best You Can Be –
Doc Susie Anderson

In 1875, Doc Susie was five years old and her brother was three when their mother left and their parents were divorced. Their grandmother moved in to help raise them, and she told them that they needed to work hard and be the best they could be, at whatever they did. Doc Susie certainly took those words to heart, becoming a beloved doctor in Fraser, Colorado – but not before she overcame a significant series of hardships.

When Doc Susie graduated from eighth grade, she taught at the school she had attended for the two years it took for her brother, John, to catch up to her in terms of education. Then the two went to high school together.

After her father remarried, Doc Susie did not get along with her stepmother. Although she went off to college to the University of Michigan to study medicine, her father ended up only being able to pay for her first year. The needs of his second wife and Doc Susie's stepsiblings took priority. So she borrowed money and worked to pay for her education – and she finished her degree at a time when very few women became medical doctors.

Unable to find work as a doctor, Doc Susie served as a nurse for six years in Greeley, Colorado. Stricken with tuberculosis at age thirty-eight, she relocated to Fraser, Colorado, to recover her health. Although she told no one that she was a doctor, the people in the small town found out. Her first patient was a horse that had been caught on barbed wire. Soon, she was making house calls and tending to the sick.

There were twelve houses in the town of Fraser when Doc Susie moved there. The men were quite skeptical of the woman doctor, but the women loved her. Her philosophy, simply, was that she helped sick people. The townspeople saw her as compassionate and understanding. The people were poor and often paid her in food or firewood.

Doc Susie Anderson

But Doc Susie, who had already proven her resilience, worked hard and did her best. She practiced medicine until she was eighty-four years old.

What's the Worst Thing That Can Happen? –
Jill Tietjen

Nine months after her first marriage, Jill Tietjen's mother-in-law and father-in-law died in a murder-suicide. These events actually occurred over a period of eight weeks, and in the end, three people were dead, including another man. Jill's two brothers-in-law, fourteen and eighteen years old, came to live with Jill and her first husband, who were both twenty-two at the time. Jill and her husband supported the young men through their high school and college years. They then supported the younger brother through law school, while Jill and her husband completed their own MBA degrees at night and worked, during the day, at their first engineering jobs.

To Jill, these complex and demanding situations epitomize some of the very worst circumstances that one can imagine facing. These experiences have framed Jill's decision-making processes and shaped the ways in which she advises others, as they face difficult life situations. When an obstacle occurs, she advises others to imagine and think about things this way: "What is the worst thing – and the worst outcome – that could happen? What would you do if it *does* really happen?" She helps them develop resilience.

In almost every case, the worst possible thing doesn't actually happen. But, since you have prepared for the very worst thing, you are now overprepared for anything else that might happen

and that might come your way. And, the
actual thing that happens will usually
never be as bad as the situation you
have imagined and for which you
have prepared. In this case, over-
preparation is a valuable thing.

Jill Tietjen

If Not Me, Who? –
Mary Lou Makepeace

Mary Lou Makepeace was sixteen years old when her father was killed in an accident on the railroad where he worked. Her sister was twelve. Her mother was incapacitated with grief – and pregnant. As the oldest child, all of the responsibilities of the household fell to Mary Lou. If she didn't do it, who would?

And shoulder those responsibilities she did. Demonstrating her resilience, Mary Lou made sure that her sister was fed, had adequate clothing, got to school on time, and that she continued on with her life and activities. Mary Lou also took care of her baby sister when she arrived. And she herself went to school and continued with her studies as well.

Mary Lou says she had a great teacher in high school who told her that she had to get away and go to college, that she couldn't be the adult in the family anymore, and that she should live her own life. And fortunately, Mary Lou's mother was able to step back into her appropriate maternal role, and Mary Lou did go to college.

She says the lessons she learned from these early life experiences included "having a realistic view" of life, and that life is not everything you might want it to be. Her early life also taught her not to give up easily. Now, she always looks for the lesson in any experience or situation. She says that, mainly, what her early life experiences taught her was that she was in charge of herself. That's pretty much how she is today. She knows that "if it isn't her, who would it be?"

Mary Lou Makepeace

I Lost My Rock –
Bee Harris

The night before Election Day in 2008, Bee Harris received the most distressing call of her life. Her mother had been murdered – and the murder suspect was a member of her extended family. Bee had lost her "rock." What had promised to be one of the most exciting times of her life – the election of the first African American president, Barack Obama – instead became a time of mourning.

Bee's mother and father were high school sweethearts who married when they were seventeen years old and then dropped out of high school. By the time they were twenty-seven, they had six children. They instilled in their children the value of education. Bee's father graduated from high school along with one of his sons by going to night school. Her mother eventually got her GED. Bee's parents also instilled in their children the value of hard work. But life was not only work. Every day when Bee and her siblings got home from school, they found ice cream money so they could have an after-school treat.

Bee has already honored, and is continuing to honor, her mother, her rock, in several ways. First, Bee published a tribute to her mother in her newspaper the *Urban Spectrum*. Second, she is planning to start a bed and breakfast that will be called "Big Ma's Place." Third, she is writing a book about her mother entitled *The Story of Ruth*. And, fourth, she is planning to launch the Ruth Boyd

Elder Abuse Foundation. These elaborate plans reflect the love, admiration, and respect that Bee feels for her rock, her deceased mother.

Bee Harris

Bee's resilience and determination shine through her many activities. She said that she has learned that "life is short" and that everyone needs to learn to appreciate life, as well as your own family and the people around you. Although she has lost her "rock," Bee continues to live a good life, always honoring her mother by succeeding herself.

CHAPTER 9

Action-Orientation

Action is epitomized by the Nike slogan "Just Do It!" It means taking steps to do something – typically to achieve an objective. It means not waiting for someone else to do it but instead taking the bull by the horns. It generally means that the person taking the action also takes personal responsibility for the results of that action.

Taking action is not always easy. It usually means a lot of hard work. It means saying you'll do something and then following through and honoring your commitments. Sometimes, maybe often, it means doing the tasks that others don't want to handle. It involves an attitude of "everything is my job." It requires putting one foot in front of the other and keeping on keeping on. Action-oriented people do not wallow.

Action – and the work associated with it – was summarized by Thomas Jefferson as follows: "I am a great believer in luck, and I find the harder I work, the more I have of it." The women in this chapter could never be accused of having idle hands – they took action to ensure that what they wanted to see happen, happened.

The Greatest Athlete to Ever Live –
Babe Didrikson Zaharias

From a very young age, Babe Didrikson Zaharias set herself a goal – she was going to be the "greatest athlete to ever live." She certainly came close to achieving her goal, widely touted today as the "greatest female athlete in history."

Called a tomboy as she was growing up, Babe (nicknamed after Babe Ruth because she could hit home runs as a kid), excelled in every sport she played. In high school, those sports included volleyball, tennis, baseball, basketball, and swimming. In the late 1920s, she was recruited to play basketball on a corporate team and achieved All-American status. By then, she had also turned her attention to track and field. At the 1932 Olympics in Los Angeles, women were allowed to compete in only three events. Babe chose three track-and-field events to compete in and won two gold medals and one silver.

Babe eventually turned her attention to golf, where she also excelled. From 1934 on, her athletic attentions were focused exclusively on golf. She hit up to one thousand balls every day, took lessons for hours, and played so much that her hands bled – the epitome of action-orientation! In 1947, Babe won seventeen straight golf championships. In 1950, she was one of the founders of the Ladies Professional Golf Association (LPGA). Combining the tournaments she won as both an amateur and professional, the total is an astounding eighty-two. She still holds the LPGA record for being the first person to accumulate ten wins, twenty wins, and thirty wins in the least amount of time. Babe was named "Female Athlete of the Year" six times by the Associated Press.

Babe Didrikson Zaharias

As the woman who said, "All my life, I've had the urge to do things better than anyone else," Babe followed through. She strove all her life for her goal of being the greatest athlete to have ever lived.

You Have to Prove Your Mettle –
Morley Ballantine

Morley Ballantine understood that when you run a newspaper in a small town like Durango, Colorado, and you weren't born in that small town, you have to prove your mettle and make a contribution. And prove it she did.

She and her husband ensured the editorial quality of the *Durango Herald*. She wrote a weekly column, an advice column, and frequent editorials – signed with her initials MCB. Today, the paper is still in the family, continuing to build on the strong foundation that she established.

The Ballantines were significant supporters of the arts and education in their community. The Ballantine Family Fund gave grants to nonprofit organizations that would make life better in Southwest Colorado, and the fund was often the leader in setting direction for other grants and organizations. One example is the Journey of Hope, which raises money for mammograms for women who can't afford them. Morley and the Ballantine Family Fund were first in line – demonstrating faith and courage in that effort and leading others to support it. Morley said, "Fulfill the community needs that you see and esteem, not what somebody else wants."

Fort Lewis College, its Center of Southwest Studies, and the Durango Arts Center were just a few of the organizations that benefited from Morley's dedication to the community. That dedication was recognized when she became the first woman to receive an honorary degree from Fort Lewis College.

Morley understood her civic obligations, but more than that, she knew that in order for the newspaper and the family to be accepted in the small town of Durango, Colorado, she needed to take action and prove her mettle.

Morley Ballantine

A Working Woman I Will Be –
Ellie Miller Greenberg

Ellie Miller Greenberg's life was turned upside down during her first semester in college. Her heretofore "perfect" life was torn apart by her parents' divorce. To Ellie, her parents' divorce announcement was a total surprise. Neither she, nor her sister, nor her mother were prepared to handle her father's surprise announcement that he wanted a divorce . . . and that he planned to marry another woman whom he had met recently at a party. Everyone in the family was totally unprepared for this situation – unprepared emotionally, professionally, and financially.

The ramifications of the divorce changed the trajectory of Ellie's life. She saw that her mother, who was left without financial security, was not prepared to earn a living. Ellie decided that she would never be in that situation. After graduating from Mount Holyoke College, she went on to graduate school at the University of Wisconsin, received her master's degree in speech pathology, and then accepted a job offer to work with brain-injured children, which gave her a chance to move to Denver, Colorado. This allowed her to leave her family's divorce drama behind in New Jersey and start a new life in a new place.

It became clear to Ellie that any man she would marry would need to understand her desire to have a career, as well as have a marriage and a family. That was not the norm in the early 1950s. Ellie knew that she needed to have a career that could provide for her financial independence, and that she needed to find a husband who would agree to have a working wife. Not only was that not the norm, but there were no role models for that kind of life in 1954! But Ellie was determined to have a career where she could work independently and earn a living. And she wanted a marriage that did not require her to live under

Ellie Miller Greenberg

the specter of divorce. That was a tall order.

Ellie thrived in her career, found a wonderfully supportive man to marry, raised three independent children, and remained the exception among her socioeconomic peers. She put into action the lessons she learned from observing the difficulties her mother had experienced after her divorce. Thus, even without role models or mentors during the 1950s and 1960s, Ellie set the pace for other women who were learning how to successfully combine having a family with an independent and demanding professional career.

Making Lemonade Out of Lemons –
Jo Ann Joselyn

Jo Ann Joselyn didn't let a "no" stop her. She believes that no actually propelled her to say yes to the opportunity of a lifetime. She made lemonade out of that lemon.

Jo Ann spent the majority of her career in the Civil Service of the US government. She was a research scientist who forecasted space weather. In her fifties, she decided she would apply for training for the Senior Executive Service. This is a special branch of the Civil Service where, once you are trained, you are on call to fill higher levels of service in the US government. For example, you might be asked to serve as an interim director of a laboratory until a permanent director is selected. The application process for this type of role was very involved, and Jo Ann completed her part. But the director of the laboratory where she worked told her he would not process her application – because he didn't think she was "that kind of material." Ironically, that lemon would lead to lemonade.

Soon after, the phone rang. In that conversation, Jo Ann was asked to put her name in as the US candidate for the secretary-general of the International Union of Geodesy and Geophysics. She of course said yes! Jo Ann believes that going through the rejection associated with the Senior Executive Service application process set her up for the action of saying yes to this new opportunity.

Jo Ann says she leaped at the chance, even though "she believed she wouldn't get it." The position was an elected one and everyone "knew" that the Canadian nominee (nominees are put forth by countries, which then provide the financial support for the person selected to be in the position) would win. Jo Ann thought that she was just a throwaway candidate. She says that she even filled out the application in crayon!

Jo Ann Joselyn

But the Canadian nominee had to withdraw when Canada withdrew the funding for that position. No other country had submitted a nomination except the United States, and Jo Ann was elected.

She says that being in that position was a tremendous opportunity and a wonderful time in her life. She didn't see the "no" as an obstacle; rather, she saw it more as a turning point. She made lemonade out of that lemon – and ended up saying yes to an even greater opportunity.

Jumping in with Both Feet –
Merle Chambers

Merle Chambers didn't have the time or opportunity to think twice when top management left the family business. She and her husband had to jump in with both feet immediately, take action, and get the company functioning and financially stable.

Merle was trained as an attorney and said that until this crisis happened, she had spent her time as either a perpetual graduate student or as a lawyer. But the business challenge she and her husband now faced was enormous, and there was no choice. She was an only child, and the business was her inheritance.

Merle had learned business concepts growing up at her parents' dinner table; her mother and father had started a transportation business just before World War II. When her father volunteered to serve in the military during the war and was sent to England, her mother had to run the business, which was still in start-up mode and not making much money.

Merle's mother was not her only role model in handling difficult situations, however. Her mother's mother was widowed twice before she was forty and had to raise her children alone. Her father's mother was a divorced schoolteacher who ensured that all of her children were educated. Merle says that there is a long family history of strong women who modeled the way for her.

Merle says that it was energizing and exhausting to take over the family business. She was coming into a business that was not well-run, and all the top management was gone. So she relied on her instinct. She had all types of responsibility that she hadn't had before, and she found out that she actually knew what she was doing and that she could do the job. She just did what was put in front of her. And, she learned and learned and learned.

Merle Chambers

She learned to hire people. She learned to listen to the employees. She learned to ask others' opinions before she stated her own. She learned to be open and to get the answers she needed. She learned to treat people well. She learned about when it was time to let people go who were unhappily employed.

Merle likens this challenging experience to "having a neutron bomb going off." There was a challenge and a problem in front of her and she did what she had to do – she jumped in with both feet!

Don't Go Through Life as a Cow – *Arlene Hirschfeld*

Arlene Hirschfeld heeded her father's advice to not "go through life as a cow that just chews its cud and gives milk." She has lived a life of philanthropy and generosity of spirit that has left a large legacy, in spite of the heartbreaks she has faced along the way.

After five funerals in three years, including that of her father and her infant son, Arlene says her perspective became "to live every day, appreciate what you can, try to be the best person that you can be, try to like everyone and find good in everybody." As a result of these experiences, Arlene poured herself into the volunteer world at a time when women were beginning to enter the workforce in large numbers.

Through these difficult experiences, Arlene learned that no one had the perfect life – the perfect partner, the perfect house, and the perfect kids. During this time, the importance of family was reinforced for her. And, she learned that women *can* do it all, just not all at the same time.

Many years later, on a trip to Hawaii, an errant umbrella further solidified these perspectives for her. The umbrella landed on her during a gust of wind – causing her to have multiple back surgeries and multiple surgeries on a shattered finger. Arlene says that the personal heartbreaks and the umbrella incident taught her to "think about the worst thing you can relate to" and, then, to "understand that many problems in life are truly minor."

Arlene has given her time and talent to a wide array of organizations, including the Women's Foundation of Colorado, the Denver Art Museum, the Junior League of Denver, and the Rose Community Foundation, to name just a few. She has made sure that she took action and was "not going through her life as a cow," as her

Arlene Hirschfeld

father had reminded her. Rising above her heartbreak, she did not just "chew her cud and give milk" – she made a real difference for countless people.

I Always Do the Hardest Thing –
Terri Finkel

Terri Finkel says when faced with a choice, she always does the hardest thing. And when she sets the standard she wants to achieve in accomplishing that hardest thing – it is set very high. In retrospect, her grandmother's experiences influenced Terri to always do the hardest thing.

Terri's grandmother had a successful clothing business in Germany before World War II. Forced to sell that business as the family made plans to flee, she nevertheless lost the money from the sale during those chaotic days. When the family moved to Shanghai, she set up a new clothing business in the American Quarter, and that business was also successful. But the Japanese capture of Shanghai meant that all the Jews were moved into a ghetto, and again Terri's grandmother established a clothing business. Then, when the family finally settled in Minnesota, yes, she did it again – a successful clothing business in the United States!

Given her family history of persistence in the face of adversity and taking action, the bar had been set very high for Terri: she had the expectation that she would always undertake the hardest thing – and succeed. And so she did. Terri combined a medical practice with medical research, with a happy and loving marriage, and with raising children. Along the way, she fortunately had lots of support – from her husband, from her mother, and from mentors. Nevertheless, she was exhausted and struggling to combine effectively what she characterizes as two careers – medical practice and medical research – not wanting to give up either one. And once, when she did give up the medical research activities, she found it to be calling her again – and so she returned.

Many years later, Terri says the push-pull of medical practice and research is still there, but she has

Terri Finkel

accepted it. She has also learned to set boundaries and to say no. Even today, she still sets the bar very high – and still expects herself to "always do the hardest thing."

CHAPTER 10

Passion

Passion is a strong feeling of enthusiasm or excitement for something or about doing something. In fact, the type of passion exhibited by the women in this chapter, and many of the other women in this book, is a driving life force.

People driven by passion feel compelled to follow specific objectives or goals in their lives. They understand they may have to do it without anyone else. They pursue this passion in spite of people telling them not to. They were not deterred when told that people, particularly women, can't succeed doing what they are doing. They persevere when told that what they want to accomplish isn't possible. They persist even when they feel at times they are alone. They are steadfast in their pursuit through ill health, difficult economies, and World Wars. They don't stop when others don't understand why they keep pushing forward. Their quest might at times lead others in society to even consider them "crazy."

Passion is epitomized in these words from an opera director, "I don't do opera because I want to. I do opera because I *have* to." These women had to act the way they did and move in the directions in which they moved. They had to follow their passion. Their passion is their raison d'être.

Mother of Charities –
Frances Wisebart Jacobs

A founder of what is known today as the United Way, Frances Wise-bart Jacobs told the *Rocky Mountain News* in 1888, "I know that whenever women lead in good work, men will follow." She knew that many poverty-stricken and ill people were in the community and that they needed to be helped. The organizations she founded out of her passion to help – United Way and National Jewish Hospital – led her to be called today the "Mother of Charities."

Frances couldn't ignore the suffering around her. As president of the Hebrew Ladies Benevolent Society, she administered to the Russian Jewish refugees and ill Jewish consumptives (those with tuberculosis) in Denver. When she saw that the problem was more widespread than just in the Jewish community, she founded the nonsectarian Denver Ladies' Relief Society in 1874. Serving as an officer in that organization, she spoke widely about the need for a concerted community-wide effort to address unmet needs. In 1887, she was one of the founders of the nation's first successful, federated, charitable organization – Charity Organization Society. Today, it is known nationally as the United Way.

But Frances wasn't done. She worked on behalf of homeless women, urged better standards for all working women, and lobbied successfully for separate quarters for women in prisons. After she spoke in San Francisco and saw a kindergarten there, she came back

to Denver and advocated for free kinder-
gartens – also successfully.

Her work on behalf of consumptives also left a lasting legacy.
She worked to raise money for a
hospital, which opened in 1892.
After her death at the age of forty-nine, also in 1892, the hospital
was named in her honor. The financial panic of 1893 forced the hospital
to close, but it reopened in 1899 as
National Jewish Hospital. Today,

Frances Wisehart Jacobs

it is called the National Jewish Center for Immunology and Respi-
ratory Medicine and is world famous.

In 1899, the "Mother of Charities" was fittingly honored in
the Colorado State Capitol. Sixteen stained glass windows adorn
the capitol dome – fifteen men and one woman – Frances Wise-
bart Jacobs.

Opportunity and Soup –
Emily Griffith

Emily Griffith lived by the motto "For Those Who Wish to Learn" and felt compelled to provide people with opportunities to achieve their learning and educational dreams. Although she was not provided with the opportunity to attend and graduate from high school herself, the lessons she learned about the importance of education fueled her passion and determination to become a teacher, to establish a school for adults, and to ensure that those adults had every opportunity to learn – by setting long school hours and even providing soup.

Emily's family was very poor, and her sister, Florence, had a mental illness. Emily was only able to attend school through the eighth grade, after which she needed to take care of her family. At sixteen years old, she had to go to work – after the economy crashed in 1884 and money was even more scarce than before, and her family needed additional income. Surprisingly, she convinced the Broken Bow, Nebraska, School Board to hire her. She had acquired much of her knowledge on her own, and she had passed all the tests the school board had given to her.

Emily learned to teach by teaching her students. She also realized that her students' parents were often illiterate, and she believed that the parents could benefit from education as well. After her family moved to Denver in 1895, she was able to do something about this situation.

Emily was hired by the Denver Public Schools, even after she told them that she was only fifteen years old and had no teaching experience. This was because although she was actually twenty-seven years old and had eleven years of teaching experience (she looked very young for her age her whole life), she had little formal education and no higher education and thus didn't have the qualifications that Denver Public Schools expected for their teachers. She worked her way all the way up from being an alternate (substitute) teacher to becoming the assistant state superintendent. But her love remained in teaching. And her dream of a school for adults also remained with her.

Emily Griffith

In 1916, the Denver School Board endorsed Emily's idea of an Opportunity School for adults, and the school opened that September. Emily had hoped to have two hundred students, but fourteen hundred adult students registered during the first week! Open from morning to night, the school was a big success. And, after one student fainted in class because he didn't have enough time to eat between work and school, Emily began providing soup – almost two hundred bowls of soup were served every day.

After her retirement, the school was renamed the Emily Griffith Opportunity School. Today, the school is called Emily Griffith Technical College. Emily Griffith's dream of creating learning opportunities for adults continues to this day, as many forms of adult education thrive in the twenty-first century.

Music Doesn't Hurt Little Girls –
Antonia Brico

Abused by the foster parents who brought her from the Netherlands to the United States, and who raised her but never adopted her, future conductor Antonia Brico would say, as she played the piano, "Music doesn't hurt little girls."

Determined to become a conductor at a time when such a thing was unheard of for women, Antonia moved to Europe to study conducting in 1923. In 1930, she made her conducting debut (as guest conductor) to great praise with the Berlin Philharmonic. But at that time, full-time jobs for women conductors simply didn't exist.

She would have to make her own jobs! Returning to the United States in 1934, Antonia founded the Women's Symphony Orchestra in New York City to prove that women could play all instruments – and could, indeed, conduct. She found support from a broad range of individuals, including Eleanor Roosevelt. In 1938, she became the first woman to conduct the New York Philharmonic Orchestra.

She settled in Denver in 1942 with the objective of auditioning for and winning the position of conductor of the Denver Symphony Orchestra, but the job went to a man. Antonia believed that she had been born fifty years too early to secure the opportunities for which she was qualified.

During World War II, she had more conducting opportunities – because the men were involved in the war effort. After the war, however, Antonia again had to found her own orchestra in order to conduct. Today, that orchestra is the Denver Philharmonic Orchestra. In addition to her conducting, Antonia gave piano and voice lessons.

Antonia Brico

Antonia has been featured in an Oscar-nominated documentary, *Antonia: A Portrait of the Woman*, which has been selected for preservation at the National Film Registry of the Library of Congress. In 2019, Antonia was the subject of a feature-length movie entitled *The Conductor*. Antonia never let obstacles stop her from pursuing her conducting passion. She knew in her heart that "music doesn't hurt little girls."

She Picked the Shortest Line –
Marion Downs

Newborn hearing screening is performed universally today, and it can be traced back to Marion Downs's decision to pursue graduate work in speech pathology and audiology at the University of Denver – because "it had the shortest line."

Already the mother of three children at the time she enrolled in graduate school, Marion earned her master's degree in audiology and began a career that resulted in her being called the "Mother of Pediatric Audiology." In the 1950s, when she began fitting children as young as six months old with hearing aids, Marion was going against the conventional treatment modes of the day. Leading pediatricians and otolaryngologists were opposed to her practice, and some audiologists even told her that hearing aids would harm children at such a young age.

Marion knew from her own experience that the leading clinicians were wrong. During the 1960s, she pioneered the first large-scale infant hearing screening program – seventeen thousand babies were tested. Then, for the next thirty years, she worked to have the hearing of all babies tested, regardless of where they were born. Her dedication to the cause of early infant hearing testing included the formation of a committee in 1969 that would eventually establish protocols and guidelines for infant testing and intervention. Finally, research published in 1993 and 1995 validated her findings that early intervention and treatment were sound and effective. Newborn hearing screening then became a universal reality.

Marion's passion for newborn hearing screening has positively changed the lives of many individuals with hearing loss. And it all came about because "she picked the shortest line."

Marion Downs

No Dogs or Mexicans Allowed –
Polly Baca

Polly Baca traces her passion to change bigotry and racial prejudice back to when she was three years old. Her family attended the only Catholic church in Greeley, Colorado. One Sunday morning, Polly saw little girls all dressed in white so they could march around the church. She wanted to sit in the center aisle so she could see them go around. She pestered her parents until the family moved and sat in the center aisle. Almost immediately, an usher came over and told them they would have to move – the church was segregated, and Mexican Americans had to sit in the side aisles only – they were not allowed in the center aisle.

Polly knew this was wrong. It made her feel that she was "less than." And that feeling was reinforced by signs in store windows in Greeley that said, "No Dogs or Mexicans Allowed." But from that pain of bigotry came her mission. She began to think there was a burden on her shoulders, and that she was going to change the racial inequality she began to see all around her. It was her responsibility.

Polly studied in elementary school. She studied in high school – the laboratory school at what now is the University of Northern Colorado. She qualified for a joint scholarship and used it to attend Colorado State University. She was always motivated by having to be "better than" in order to be "just as good as."

Her list of firsts became long and impressive. She was the first college student to win a statewide office in the Young Democrats. She was the first woman and the first Mexican American to edit a labor union newspaper. She was the first woman in a professional position in the Democratic National Committee for Bobby Kennedy's presidential campaign. And she was the cochair of the Democratic National Convention in 1980 and 1984.

Polly Baca

All of those achievements (and many more) came from a woman who says, "The greatest gift God ever gave me was being born a female child to a poor Mexican American family in a bigoted community." This is a woman who took signs that said, "No Dogs or Mexicans Allowed" as a personal challenge and made it her responsibility to prove that she and her community were "as good as."

Conclusion

All of the Hall of Famers whose stories are presented herein experienced significant challenges and obstacles over the course of their lifetimes. Any one of these challenges might have defeated or destroyed any ordinary human being. These challenges were not trivial. Although some were among the ordinary challenges of life, others were unusual or the result of historic circumstances.

Challenges can defeat or strengthen. But they cannot be ignored.

The challenges they faced ranged from the horrific to the tragic, and included

- Slavery
- Death of their mother
- Death of their father
- Divorce of their parents
- Illness
- Bigotry – prejudice – discrimination
- Murder or murder-suicide in their family
- Incest
- Abusive environments

... and many more.

Each of us has probably experienced at least one of these challenges. We know from our own experience that any one of these life-defining events could either stop us in our tracks or become a significant challenge from which we learned and from which we grew stronger.

By examining and analyzing the lives of the remarkable and achieving women in this book, we have identified ten key characteristics, or circumstances, that have been present and have been, in many cases, responsible for their success in overcoming the challenges and obstacles they met throughout their lifelong journeys.

They surmounted the obstacles and challenges they encountered by using one or more of the ten key characteristics we have identified:

1. Mental Intelligence
2. Emotional Intelligence
3. Social Support
4. Moral Compass – Spirituality
5. Determination – Perseverance – Persistence
6. Optimism
7. Creativity
8. Resilience
9. Action-Orientation
10. Passion

Key "themes for success" emerged that often were repeated from Hall of Famer to Hall of Famer. These themes demonstrate philosophies these women adopted to face the numerous and significant obstacles in their lives. They are:

- Say yes to opportunity.
- Do your very best in everything you do.
- Work hard.

- Never give up.
- Remember that the only thing you can control in life is your attitude.

Imagine a room with five posters on the walls . . . one poster containing each of the five above themes. The letters are painted in bright colors, while the background paper is white. Now, imagine a young teenager decorating her room with those five posters. She would see them every day as she grew up. By the end of her teenage years, those five themes would have been embedded in her mind, memorized, and become part of her philosophy of life. What a difference those five themes . . . those five big ideas . . . could make!

We hope these personal stories, the lessons they teach, and the themes of a successful life we have distilled from these journeys will resonate with every reader. We also hope that each reader will take away from this book at least one "nugget" that will help them personally with the life challenges they inevitably will face.

Remember: none of us will go through life unscathed.

For, without obstacles, there is no life.

Biographical Notes

The first woman in the United States to receive a professional jockey's license, **Anna Lee Aldred** (1921–2006) raced from 1939 until 1945, when she grew too big to be a jockey. Anna Lee loved horses and started riding and racing them as a young girl. She became a rodeo trick rider after retiring from professional racing. Until she broke her hip at age eighty, Anna Lee continued to assist jockeys at fairgrounds and races.

One of the first women to practice medicine in Colorado, **Doc Susie Anderson** (1869–1960) moved to Fraser in 1907. During the 1918 flu epidemic, she was in great demand due to her reputation for saving pneumonia patients. For forty-nine years, she treated every patient who needed her, including animals, assisting in childbirth, and ministering to lumberjacks, railroad workers, ranchers, and skiers at Winter Park. Doc Susie became beloved by the townspeople.

Lena Archuleta (1920–2011) was the first Latina principal in the Denver Public Schools. Over more than thirty years, she advocated for the Latino community in educational institutions and was the first woman to serve as president of the Latin American Education Foundation. Lena was the first Latina president of the Denver Classroom Teachers' Association and the Colorado Library Association. She helped found the Circle of Latina Leadership.

Christine Arguello (1955–) was the first Latino US district court judge for the District of Colorado. Her many firsts include the first Latina from Colorado to be admitted to Harvard Law School, the first Latina to be tenured and promoted to full professor at the University of Kansas School of Law, the first Latina to be elected to the Board of Education for Colorado Springs School District 11, and the first Latino chief deputy attorney general for Colorado.

The 1958 Miss America, **Marilyn Van Derbur Atler** (1937–) stunned the world when, as an adult, she revealed that she was an incest survivor. A nationally known and loved motivational speaker for years, Marilyn used the skills honed in that speaking to travel the United States and the globe advocating for survivors of sexual assault and incest. Her book, *Miss America by Day*, provides hope for survivors and those who help survivors.

The first Latina elected to the Colorado Senate, **Polly Baca** (1941–) has a long list of firsts. Fueled by her determination from age three to overcome discrimination, she is a strong advocate for Latinx and gender equity. Her firsts include the first Latina to chair the Democratic National Convention, the first Latina to receive a major party nomination for the US Congress, and the first woman to chair the Democratic Caucus in the Colorado House of Representatives.

Born into a newspaper publishing family, **Morley Ballantine** (1925–2009) served as co-owner, publisher, principal editor, and writer for the *Durango Herald*. She led the newspaper as chair of the board and was the first female chair of the Colorado Press Association. Morley wrote about local, national, and international issues and advocated for reproductive rights as well as gender equity. She helped direct the activities of the Ballantine Family Fund, which improved arts and education in Southwest Colorado.

Pianist and conductor **Antonia Brico** (1902–1989) was the first American accepted into the Berlin State Academy of Music where she graduated from its master class in conducting. After debuting with the Berlin Philharmonic Orchestra, she founded the Women's Symphony Orchestra in New York City. During her career, Antonia was not able to overcome overt discrimination against women conductors as documented in the Academy Award–nominated documentary, *Antonia: A Portrait of the Woman.*

The first Black woman to cross the Plains during the Gold Rush, **Clara Brown** (1800–1885) was born a slave. She lived in Central City, Colorado, where she established a laundry, expanded her business ventures, made investments with the money she earned, and spent many years of her life looking for her family members. The "Angel of the Rockies" was dedicated to strong communities and was generous with her philanthropy. "Aunt" Clara relocated a number of family members to Colorado and eventually found her daughter who had been sold to a different owner at auction forty-seven years before.

Philanthropist and women's advocate **Merle Chambers** (1946–) was a founding board member of the Women's Foundation of Colorado and was instrumental in the establishment of the Chambers Center for the Advancement of Women at the University of Denver. Active in civic, cultural, and philanthropic affairs, Merle earlier pioneered women's leadership in the oil and gas industry as CEO of an independent oil and gas exploration and production company.

One of the first Latinas to earn a PhD in Colorado, **Sister Alicia Cuarón**'s (1939–) other firsts include first Latina to serve as executive director of the Colorado Economic Development Association, first Latina to serve as Colorado State Fair commissioner, and first woman executive director of the National Hispanic Association of Construction Enterprises. Sister Alicia entered the Sisters of Saint Francis when she was in her fifties, dedicating her efforts since to providing educational opportunities and social services to many immigrant and low income families.

The "Mother of Pediatric Audiology," **Marion Downs** (1914–2014) fought tirelessly for newborn infant hearing screening and early intervention for those with hearing issues. Going against the wisdom of the day, she fitted infants with hearing aids as young as six months. After four decades of her advocacy, hearing screening for newborns was adopted universally. Marion was also a prolific author of journal articles, chapters in books, and books. An advocate of an active lifestyle, she skied until she was ninety-five.

The first successful African American businesswoman in Colorado Springs, **Fannie Mae Duncan** (1918–2005) ran the Haven Club, a soda fountain for Black soldiers stationed at Fort Carson during World War II. She also operated a USO concession. After the war, Fannie Mae founded the integrated Cotton Club, a jazz mecca in Colorado Springs that attracted luminaries from across the country. Her embrace of everyone in the community led to the peaceful integration of the city.

Dr. Terri Finkel's (1952–) research in immunology and clinical applications has enhanced our knowledge of autoimmunity,

AIDS, juvenile rheumatoid arthritis, lupus, and cancer. During her career, Terri has worked at National Jewish Health, the University of Pennsylvania School of Medicine, and Le Bonheur Children's Hospital, among others. Renowned as a pediatric rheumatologist and immunologist, Terri's work has been highlighted on the cover of *Rolling Stone* magazine, and her biography has been read into the *Congressional Record*.

Denver's first Black woman physician, **Dr. Justina Ford** (1871–1952) specialized in gynecology, obstetrics, and pediatrics. Precluded from practicing at the hospital due to her race, Justina treated people of color as well as "plain white" people (immigrants and those in lower socioeconomic classes) from her home or by making house calls. She learned multiple foreign languages so that she could communicate with her patients. Over the course of her fifty-year career in Denver, Justina delivered more than seven thousand babies

As CEO and medical director of Denver Health and Hospital Authority, **Dr. Patty Gabow** (1944–) was nationally recognized for increasing health-care access for all citizens of Colorado, especially the underserved, who are primarily women and children. Patty led the effort to convert the former Denver General Hospital to a community-owned authority, not a unit of the City of Denver. An expert in kidney disease, she is also an author and speaker.

There wouldn't be a Colorado Trail if there hadn't been **Gudy Gaskill** (1927–2016). For twenty-five years, she worked to make her dream a reality. At more than five hundred miles long, the Colorado Trail is one of the premiere recreational attractions in the state.

An experienced hiker and climber, Gudy recruited volunteers from around the country – and the world – to build the trail one segment at a time. The Colorado Trail has become a model project for other states and agencies to emulate.

Half of the cattle in the United States and Canada live in facilities designed by animal scientist and autism spokesperson and advocate **Dr. Temple Grandin** (1947–). An advocate for humane treatment of animals, Temple has worked at Colorado State University for more than twenty-five years. A movie has been made of her life, she has authored many books, she has been named a "Hero" by *Time* magazine, and she speaks around the world on the topic of autism.

Because she believed that education is the key to social change and social justice and in access for all, **Ellie Miller Greenberg** (1932–2021) was a leader in adult education and adult development. She served as the founding director of University Without Walls. Later, she established education programs in Colorado prisons, developed degree programs for Native American mental health workers, established a weekend nursing degree program, and established online degree programs for health-care workers. Ellie worked extensively for fair housing.

In 1916, due to **Emily Griffith**'s (1880–1947) advocacy, Denver Public Schools opened the Opportunity School to provide basic adult education and marketing skills free of charge. Emily, who had taught since she was thirteen years old, realized that the parents of the poor students she taught needed to learn enough skills to earn a living. In 1933, it was named the Emily Griffith Opportunity School and today is the Emily Griffith Technical College.

Educator and advocate for the Latina community **Maria Guajardo** (1959–) was born to illiterate Mexican migrant workers. She has committed herself to improving the lives of children and has advocated to keep children in school by understanding why they drop out, worked for world peace, and advocated for children in third world countries. She has been active in youth development as well as issues related to Latino education and health care.

Aviation pioneer **Dr. Penny Hamilton** (1948–), also known as "Penny the Pilot," co-holds a World Aviation Speed Record. She is passionate about getting more women into aviation and science, technology, engineering, and mathematics (STEM) careers. Penny was a dental hygienist and an army wife before taking up flying. An author and photographer, she educates children about aviation, writes about Grand County, Colorado, and is the director of the Teaching Women to Fly Research Project.

Bee Harris (1950–) is dedicated to providing a voice and telling the stories of communities of color. Bee founded the *Denver Urban Spectrum* newspaper, which delivers information and showcases voices not heard in the mainstream media. Bee also established the Urban Spectrum Youth Foundation to provide mentoring and training programs in the field of journalism for youth aged thirteen through seventeen.

Josie Heath (1937–) directed the Women's Center at Red Rocks Community College and has received three presidential appointments. She was the Democratic Party's nominee for US Senate from Colorado in 1990 and 1992. Josie helped establish the Women's Foundation of Colorado, served as a Boulder county commissioner and, for many years, was president of the Community Foundation serving Boulder County.

The first military woman in space, Lieutenant General and astronaut **Susan Helms** (1958–) was also the first woman to serve on the International Space Station. She graduated from the Air Force Academy in the first class that included women. She retired after a more than thirty-year air force career, during which she was the first female commander of the Cape Canaveral Air Force Station and achieved additional firsts. Helms flew on five Space Shuttle missions and conducted the longest space walk for a female astronaut.

Arlene Hirschfeld's (1944–) activism and philanthropy are fueled by her belief in the power of volunteerism to enhance the quality of life for individuals and the community. Her almost full-time volunteerism has benefited multiple organizations and causes from the Denver Art Museum to the Junior League of Denver. Nationally, she chaired the successful effort to raise funds endowing a scholar at the Harvard University Divinity School's Women's Studies in Religion Program.

The first female president of the Colorado Community College System, **Dorothy Horrell** (1951–) also served for ten years as the first woman president of Red Rocks Community College. After guiding the Bonfils-Stanton Foundation for many years, she retired only to be called to serve as chancellor at the University of Colorado at Denver. She established or helped establish two programs to advance high-potential nonprofit leaders – the Livingston Fellowship Program and the Institute for Leaders in Development.

Businesswoman **Ding-Wen Hsu** (1948–) founded the Dragon Boat Festival in Colorado, the largest Asian festival in the Rocky Mountain region, which now attracts one hundred thousand participants. An advocate in many ways for the invisible Asian communities in the state, Ding-Wen recognized the lack of leadership opportunities for Asian youth. She helped establish the Asian and Pacific Islander Emerging Leaders Program to identify and develop the next generation of Asian American leaders.

A driving force in Denver's charitable activities and organizations and the so-called Mother of Charities, **Frances Wisebart Jacobs** (1843–1892) not only helped found what is today called United Way, she also founded National Jewish Hospital. She organized and was president of the Hebrew Ladies' Benevolent Society, helped found the nonsectarian Denver Ladies' Relief Society, and established the first free kindergarten in Denver. Jacobs is the only woman featured in the sixteen stained glass windows in the Colorado Capitol dome.

Astrogeophysicist **Dr. Jo Ann Joselyn** (1943–) was the first woman secretary-general of the International Association of Geomagnetism and Aeronomy and the first woman and the first American to serve as secretary-general of the International Union of Geodesy and Geophysics. Jo Ann was the first woman to receive a doctorate from the astrogeophysics program at the University of Colorado at Boulder.

She spent her career as a space scientist whose work included forecasting space weather such as solar flares and sunspots.

Former First Lady of Colorado **Dottie Lamm** (1937–) is an author, speaker, university educator, activist, and feminist. She ran for the US Senate in 1998 after twenty years as a columnist for the *The Denver Post.* A cofounder of the Women's Foundation of Colorado, she served as its first president. She was also a founder of the Democratic Women's Caucus of Colorado. Dottie was a delegate to the Fourth Women's Conference in Beijing in 1995.

The youngest of the Little Rock Nine – the nine African American students who integrated Central High School in Little Rock, Arkansas, in 1957 – **Carlotta Walls LaNier** (1942–) wanted the best education possible, as she knew that education was the key to opportunity. She was fourteen at the time. The first female Black graduate of Central High, Carlotta is a lifelong advocate of equal education for all. She has received the Congressional Gold Medal and has been president of the Little Rock Nine Foundation.

Businesswoman **Mary Elitch Long** (1856–1936) was the only woman running an amusement park in the world. Her husband died shortly after the first season that Elitch's Zoological Gardens had been opened. For twenty years, she ran Elitch Gardens. The gardens included a zoo, and the entertainment provided included staged theater productions, movies, and live music with both brass bands and a symphony orchestra. Always looking for ways to attract customers, Mary added swings, a merry-go-round, and a train to the gardens as well.

The first woman to serve as mayor of Colorado Springs, **Mary Lou Makepeace** (1940–) advocated for equal treatment for all. After her terms, which saw the first female municipal judges appointed, she worked at the Gay and Lesbian Fund for Colorado, furthering her objectives of equality, diversity, and inclusivity. Mary Lou continues her efforts to build economically self-sufficient and strong women who pursue an education and participate in the electoral process.

The first woman naturalist to procure and prepare her own specimens, taxidermist **Martha Maxwell** (1831–1881) showed her stuffed animals and birds at the 1876 American Centennial Exhibition. She opened her own museum in Boulder and exhibited her animals and birds at the Colorado Agricultural Society Fair. The first woman to have a subspecies named after her, Martha set a new standard for natural history museums, which led to dioramas featuring animals and birds in their natural habitats.

Former fashion model **Sue Miller** (1934–2017) fought fear and public ignorance about breast cancer through the establishment of a fashion show where all models were breast cancer survivors. The Day of Caring for Breast Cancer Awareness became an annual event in cities around the country. Sue also organized Pre-Surgical Partners through which breast cancer survivors provided advice and comfort to patients with new breast cancer diagnoses. She helped convince the Colorado State Legislature to require health-care organizations to provide mammograms for women over forty.

The first female Colorado Supreme Court chief justice, **Mary Mullarkey** (1943–2021) graduated from Harvard Law School and worked for the US Department of the Interior in the Office of the Solicitor. Mary later served as solicitor general for the state of Colorado and chief legal advisor to Governor Dick Lamm. She served on the Colorado Supreme Court for a total of twenty-three years and her tenure as chief justice – twelve years – is longer than anyone else has served in that position.

The first woman in the US armed forces to achieve the rank of three-star general (lieutenant general), **Carol Mutter** (1945–) was commissioned a second lieutenant in the US Marine Corps upon her college graduation. During her more than thirty-year career in the marine corps, she became the first woman promoted to the rank of major general within that branch of the service. As a brigadier general, Carol became the first woman of general/flag rank to command a major deployable tactical command.

Rachel B. Noel (1918–2008) dedicated herself to equal education and opportunity for all. She was the first African American woman elected to public office in Colorado and the first African American elected to the Denver Public School Board. There, she advocated for school desegregation introducing what became known as the Noel Resolution – setting a timeline for total desegregation. Rachel chaired the Department of Afro-American Studies at Metropolitan State College and was elected to the University of Colorado's Board of Regents.

Through her dedication and hard work, never taking no for an answer, **LaRae Orullian** (1933–) opened up the world of banking to more women. After many years at Guaranty Bank and having finally attained the position of bank officer there, LaRae agreed to serve as the inaugural president and CEO of the Women's Bank. She has served on and chaired numerous corporate boards as well as the World Association of Girl Guides and Girl Scouts.

Sister Lydia Peña (1934–), a Sister of Loretto, uses her fund-raising skills to provide educational opportunities for the oppressed and underserved around the world. She taught at St. Mary's Academy, Loretto Heights, and University Without Walls. Her extensive community participation includes serving on the boards of organizations as varied as the Rose Community Foundation, Rocky Mountain PBS, the Women's Forum of Colorado, and the Women's Foundation of Colorado. She has raised funds to establish a school in Ghana.

Cleo Parker Robinson (1948–) uses the power of dance to unite communities across cultures and language barriers. Her philosophy of "One Spirit, Many Voices" is evidenced in all of her activities around the world to bring joy and understanding through dance. Her Cleo Parker Robinson Dance, founded in 1970, uses dance to champion social justice and unite people across all backgrounds and ages.

Physician **Florence Sabin** (1871–1953) achieved many firsts during her career, including the first woman on the faculty at the Johns Hopkins School of Medicine, the first full woman member of the Rockefeller Institute, and the first woman elected to the National Academy of Sciences. Florence made important discoveries about the human circulatory system. After her retirement, she returned to her birthplace and lobbied successfully for the enactment of the Sabin Health Laws to improve public health in Colorado.

Pat Schroeder (1940–) represented Colorado for twelve terms in the US House of Representatives starting in 1972. She worked tirelessly to establish national family policy to address issues including parental leave, child care, family planning, and more. Pat wrote the Family and Medical Leave Act in 1985 and worked to enact legislation and secure funding for key legislation to support women's health research. Her book about her experience in Congress is titled *24 Years of House Work . . . and the Place Is Still a Mess: My Life in Politics.*

An advocate for neglected and abused children, attorney **Shari Shink** (1948–) established what became the Rocky Mountain Children's Law Center, the first nonprofit law firm for neglected/abused children. The legislative reforms that she has championed and the programs she has established help every child fulfill their potential, including those in foster care and under the supervision of juvenile court. She is most inspired by children whose lives she has been able to positively impact.

Electrical engineer **Jill S. Tietjen** (1954–) spent her career in the electric utility industry and served as an expert witness. She became the first female board member of the Rocky Mountain Electrical League and its first female president. Jill is a philanthropist, mentor, and nominator of women for professional, local, state, university, and national awards. Through her writing and speaking, she advocates for women, has worked tirelessly to increase the number of women in STEM careers, and writes women back into history.

Martha Urioste (1937–) was the first and only principal to pioneer a Montessori elementary school. The founder and former president of Family Star, Martha was a pioneering Latino American counselor in the Denver Public Schools and the first secondary bilingual counselor. Her exploration of the reason for students dropping out of high school led to her deep commitment to Montessori as an education delivery mechanism that enables students from all backgrounds to thrive and succeed.

Soil scientist and environmental ecologist **Dr. Diana Wall** (1943–) is the leading expert on soil invertebrate diversity. Her research has been focused on Antarctica where the Wall Valley was named for her. She is a university distinguished professor and served as the inaugural director of the School of Global Environmental Sustainability at Colorado State University. Her many honors include election to the National Academy of Sciences and the American Academy of Arts and Sciences.

Emily Howell Warner (1939–2020) made history by becoming the first female pilot hired by a major US airline, Frontier. Three years later, she made history again by becoming the first woman to earn her captain's wings. A role model and personal mentor to many, Emily was a flight school manager and a Federal Aviation Administration flight examiner. Her pilot's uniform is on display at the Smithsonian National Air and Space Museum.

One of the greatest athletes of all time, **Babe Didrikson Zaharias** (1911–1956) not only won three track and field medals (two gold, one silver) at the 1932 Summer Olympics, she also won ten LPGA golf championships. The Associated Press named her "Female Athlete of the Year" six times between 1932 and 1954 and "Female Athlete of the Half Century" in 1950. Babe has been featured on a US postage stamp and was awarded the Presidential Medal of Freedom posthumously.

Halls of Fame

Anna Lee Aldred
Colorado Plateau Horseman's Hall of Fame
Colorado Women's Hall of Fame
National Cowgirl Museum and Hall of Fame

Doc Susie Anderson
Colorado Women's Hall of Fame

Lena Archuleta
Colorado Women's Hall of Fame

Christine Arguello
Colorado Latino Hall of Fame
Colorado Women's Hall of Fame

Marilyn Van Derbur Atler
Colorado Authors' Hall of Fame
Colorado Women's Hall of Fame

Polly Baca
Colorado Latino Hall of Fame
Colorado Women's Hall of Fame

Morley Ballantine
Colorado Business Hall of Fame
Colorado Press Association Hall of Fame
Colorado Women's Hall of Fame

Antonia Brico
Colorado Women's Hall of Fame

Clara Brown
Colorado Women's Hall of Fame

Merle Chambers
Colorado Business Hall of Fame
Colorado Women's Hall of Fame
Rocky Mountain Oil and Gas Hall of Fame

Sister Alicia Cuarón
Colorado Latino Hall of Fame
Colorado Women's Hall of Fame

Marion Downs
Colorado Women's Hall of Fame

Fannie Mae Duncan
Colorado Women's Hall of Fame

Terri Finkel
Colorado Women's Hall of Fame

Justina Ford
Colorado Women's Hall of Fame

Patty Gabow
Colorado Women's Hall of Fame

Gudy Gaskill
Colorado Women's Hall of Fame

Temple Grandin
Colorado Women's Hall of Fame
National Women's Hall of Fame

Ellie Miller Greenberg
Colorado Women's Hall of Fame

Emily Griffith
Colorado Business Hall of Fame
Colorado Women's Hall of Fame

Maria Guajardo
Colorado Women's Hall of Fame

Penny Hamilton
Colorado Authors' Hall of Fame
Colorado Aviation Hall of Fame
Colorado Women's Hall of Fame

Bee Harris
Colorado Women's Hall of Fame

Josie Heath
Colorado Women's Hall of Fame

Susan Helms
Colorado Women's Hall of Fame
International Space Hall of Fame

Arlene Hirschfeld
Colorado Women's Hall of Fame

Dorothy Horrell
Colorado 4-H Hall of Fame
Colorado Women's Hall of Fame

Ding-Wen Hsu
Colorado Women's Hall of Fame

Frances Wisebart Jacobs
Colorado Women's Hall of Fame
National Women's Hall of Fame

Jo Ann Joselyn
Colorado Women's Hall of Fame

Dottie Lamm
Colorado Women's Hall of Fame

Carlotta Walls LaNier
Colorado Women's Hall of Fame
National Women's Hall of Fame

Mary Elitch Long
Colorado Business Hall of Fame
Colorado Women's Hall of Fame

Mary Lou Makepeace
Colorado Women's Hall of Fame

Martha Maxwell
Colorado Women's Hall of Fame

Sue Miller
Colorado Women's Hall of Fame

Mary Mullarkey
Colorado Women's Hall of Fame

Carol Mutter
Colorado Women's Hall of Fame
National Women's Hall of Fame

Rachel B. Noel
Colorado Women's Hall of Fame

LaRae Orullian
Colorado Business Hall of Fame
Colorado Women's Hall of Fame

Sister Lydia Peña
Colorado Women's Hall of Fame

Cleo Parker Robinson
Blacks in Colorado Hall of Fame
Colorado Gospel Music Academy and Hall of Fame
Colorado Women's Hall of Fame

Florence Sabin
Colorado Women's Hall of Fame
National Statuary Hall Collection, United States Capitol
National Women's Hall of Fame

Pat Schroeder
Colorado Women's Hall of Fame
National Women's Hall of Fame

Shari Shink
Colorado Women's Hall of Fame

Jill Tietjen
Colorado Authors' Hall of Fame
Colorado Women's Hall of Fame

Martha Urioste
Colorado Latino Hall of Fame
Colorado Women's Hall of Fame

Diana Wall
Colorado Women's Hall of Fame

Emily Howell Warner
Colorado Aviation Hall of Fame
Colorado Women's Hall of Fame
National Aviation Hall of Fame
National Women's Hall of Fame
Women in Aviation International Pioneer Hall of Fame

Babe Didrikson Zaharias

Colorado Golf Hall of Fame
Colorado Sports Hall of Fame
Colorado Women's Hall of Fame
Florida Sports Hall of Fame
LPGA Hall of Fame – now part of World Golf Hall of Fame
National Women's Hall of Fame
US Olympic and Paralympic Museum Hall of Fame

Bibliography

Alexander, Rachel K. "Perseverance through Change and Failure." *The Bent of Tau Beta Pi.* Summer 2020, p. 2.

Becker, Cynthia S. *Chipeta: The Peacemaker.* Palmer Lake, CO: Filter Press, LLC, 2008.

Bluemel, Elinor. *One Hundred Years of Colorado Women.* N.p.: n.p., 1973.

Cunningham, Penny. *Doc Susie: Mountain Doctor.* Palmer Lake, CO: Filter Press, LLC, 2010.

Dizik, Alina. "A Time to Build Resilience in Kids." *The Wall Street Journal.* March 27, 2020, p. R9.

Duckworth, Angela. *Grit: The Power of Passion and Perseverance.* New York: Scribner, 2016.

Ellwood, Mark. "Our Daydreams Will Save Us." *Business Week.* June 8, 2020, pp. 64–65.

Faulkner, Debra B. *Mary Elitch Long: First Lady of Fun.* Palmer Lake, CO: Filter Press, LLC, 2008.

Feiler, Bruce. "Learning to Conquer Life's Crises." *The Wall Street Journal.* July 11–12, 2020, pp. C3–4.

Griffin, Lydia. *Susan Anderson: Colorado's Doc Susie.* Palmer Lake, CO: Filter Press, LLC, 2010.

Harrar, Sari. "Happiness in Hard Times." *AARP: The Magazine.* June/July 2020, pp. 57–60.

Lohse, Joyce B. *Baby Doe Tabor: Matchless Silver Queen.* Palmer

Lake, CO: Filter Press, LLC, 2011.

Lohse, Joyce B. *Emily Griffith: Opportunity's Teacher.* Palmer Lake, CO: Filter Press, LLC, 2005.

Lohse, Joyce B. *Justina Ford: Medical Pioneer.* Palmer Lake, CO: Filter Press, LLC, 2004.

Lohse, Joyce B. *Unsinkable: The Molly Brown Story.* Palmer Lake, CO: Filter Press, LLC, 2006.

McVey, James. *Martha Maxwell: Natural History Pioneer.* Palmer Lake, CO: Filter Press, LLC, 2005.

Petersen, Andrea. "How to Build Resilience to Weather Hard Times." *The Wall Street Journal.* July 14, 2020, p. A11.

Reinstein, Mara. "Life's a Joke When You're Jerry Seinfeld. *Parade Magazine.* October 4, 2010, pp. 8–14.

Simmons, Stacey. *Florence Sabin: Scientist and Teacher.* Palmer Lake, CO: Filter Press, LLC, 2013.

Southwick, Steven M., and Dennis S. Charney. *Resilience: The Science of Mastering Life's Greatest Challenges.* Cambridge, UK: Cambridge University Press, 2018.

Varnell, Jeanne. *Women of Consequence: The Colorado Women's Hall of Fame.* Boulder, CO: Johnson Books, 1999.

Zimmerman, Eilene. "Past Experiences Make Some People More Resilient." *The Denver Post.* June 25, 2020, p. 4B.

About the Authors

Jill S. Tietjen, PE, is an author, national speaker, and electrical engineer. After more than forty-five years in the electric utility industry, her professional focus is now on women's advocacy, worldwide. Her ten books include the bestselling and award-winning *Her Story: A Timeline of the Women Who*  *Changed America* and *Hollywood: Her Story, An Illustrated History of Women and the Movies*. She has been inducted into the Colorado Women's Hall of Fame and the Colorado Authors' Hall of Fame.

Elinor Miller Greenberg, EdD, devoted her career and community life to expanding access to opportunity, especially for women and minorities, by designing and implementing innovative higher education programs for adults. She authored, coauthored, or edited nine  books and numerous articles and pamphlets. She led many academic programs and community organizations, including the University Without Walls, the Colorado Women's Leadership Coalition, and the Women's Forum of Colorado. She received multiple honorary doctorates and was inducted into the Colorado Women's Hall of Fame.

Book Club: Ten Questions and a Bonus

1. Whose story did you most relate to in the book? Why do you think that was?

2. Were you surprised to learn that women in the Colorado (and other) Women's Halls of Fame had faced obstacles – some of them extreme – in their lives? Why or why not?

3. Did the examples of Abraham Lincoln, Dr. Seuss, Madame Marie Curie, Walt Disney, and Laurie Schaefer from the foreword surprise you? Why or why not?

4. Has there been an obstacle in your life that has been what you would call a "life-defining" event? How did you handle it?

5. Will the understanding that "without obstacles, there is no life" help you as you go about your daily living? How? Why?

6. Which of the ten key characteristics for surmounting obstacles do you use in your life?

7. Is there a characteristic from the ten key characteristics that you would like to further develop in your life? How will you go about doing that?

8. What themes for success have you adopted to date in your life?

9. Which one of the keys to success described in the book will be helpful to you in the future?

10. Can you think of any people in your own life who have gone "Over, Under, Around, or Through"? How have they done that?

BONUS: Which woman/women do you think you'd like to find out more about? Why?